Introducing Children

to Folk Tales

Introducing Children

to Folk Tales

Beth Weir
Meredith College

Christopher-Gordon Publishers, Inc.
Norwood, Massachusetts

Copyright Acknowledgments

Christopher-Gordon Publishers, Inc.
1502 Providence Highway, Suite 12
Norwood, MA 02062
800-934-8322

Printed in the United States of America

10 9 8 7 6 5 4 3 2 1   05 04 03 02 01 00

Library of Congress Catalog Card Number: 99-69974
ISBN: 1-929024-16-9

Author's Note

It has been my experience as a storyteller and an teacher-educator, that teachers are very interested in folk tales but lack the time to research them. In practice, many charming retellings of folk and fairy stories are treated in the same way as other fictional genre; the focus is often on literary elements. Teachers' lack of background knowledge means that the cultural context of a given story or character, the historical significance of a tale, and the recognition of the pervasive influence on literature of folk tales is frequently ignored.

This text is an attempt to provide interested teachers with a readily accessible introductory resource on folk tales. Each chapter contains some background information on a story type or a character. An annotated bibliography of available picture books and illustrated texts written for elementary age children accompanies the introductory discussion.

Dedication

For Bruce.

About the Author

Born in New Zealand, I came to the United States in 1976 and have had a love affair with this great big country ever since.

I received my undergraduate degree in New Zealand and did my graduate work in North Carolina. For the past 12 years I have worked in the Education Department at Meredith College, one of the few remaining women's colleges in the country. Working with students who wish to become elementary teachers, I teach classes relating to literacy, reading, and writing. I also teach a class in folk lore/storytelling; I am an amateur storyteller sharing folk tales with elementary school students and teachers.

I am married with 2 grown children, an old dog, a young cat, and live in Raleigh, North Carolina.

Table of Contents

1

The Folk Tale
Tradition

Folk tales are stories of the people, the peasantry, the common folk who lived and toiled across the centuries. These simple folk are largely faceless today but they remain a vigorous presence with us through their stories.

The expression folk tale comes from the Anglo-Saxon, *talu*, which means speech in a historical sense of storytelling. It is true that many folk tales are also accounts, somewhat imperfect, but accounts nonetheless, of events of the past.

Since the tales of the people were born in antiquity and have been told and altered across time, authorship is impossible to determine. What is known is that many of the same stories appear all over the world. This is believed to have come about at least in part from periods such as the era of the Crusades across Europe from the tenth to twelfth centuries. Along with the bubonic plague the soldiers brought stories to tell around the night fire. It is not difficult to know which contribution to mankind was more desirable!

Certainly it is not hard to appreciate that stories were the currency not only of the soldiers, but also travelers, sailors, minstrels, missionaries, and pilgrims of the ages. Individual tales were enhanced and changed in numerous retellings to accommodate the particular circumstance of the telling. One example of this process is the story of four aging animal friends—a donkey, a cat, a rooster, and a dog who escape their scheming masters and take over the house of robbers. This tale is typically associated with the famous collection of the Grimm brothers of Germany. There is now a Xhosa (KOR-sa) version of this tale, firmly embedded in the folk tale traditions of that tribal group from South Africa. In the African iteration the house commandeered by the four animals is inhabited by cannibals! It is unlikely the missionaries who brought the story to the native peoples anticipated such a modification.

Kinds of Folk Tales

Folk stories are many and varied in nature but three types can be broadly distinguished: myths, legends, and stories for entertainment.

Myths. Myths or creation tales are explanatory in nature and are what author Rudyard Kipling (1978) characterizes as "Just so stories." They were told by people with little scientific knowledge as a way of making sense of the world; why there is sea and land, night and day, birds that fly south in winter, and people living upon the earth.

Legends. Legends are tales about the exploits of individuals who are frequently involved in a journey of some kind. Sometimes called hero tales, legends were inspired by an historical incident or event. As the developments of the story are much embellished by many tellings, legends can be thought of as distorted history.

Stories For Entertainment. Stories told for entertainment are commonly called folk tales or fairy tales. Such tales may have fairy-like creatures in them or simply an element of enchantment which can take many forms. Outside of the magic frequently wielded by the legendary fairy godmother, used to save the protagonist from an uncertain fate, are other forms of wonder. Frequently the characters are animals with human characteristics such as an ability to talk. The story, *Puss In Boots,* is a case in point. Through his wit the worldly cat elevates the youngest son of an impoverished miller to a comfortable and happy station. The enchantment could be also be an auspicious combination of wit, cunning, and luck. Some of the spider stories of West Africa featuring the irrepressible Anansi the Spiderman are examples of such a circumstance.

Another kind of entertainment story brought to great heights in recent times is the tall tale. These are wondrously entertaining stories that grew up, (and grew and grew), around people and their adventures while they were settling the New World. While not unknown prior to the development of North America, tall tales were firmly honed as an art form around campfires of settlers, loggers, and people on the wagon trains. Their appeal rests partly on the fact that sometimes such larger than life people existed and partly on the images created by the storyteller who considers himself an artist. Stories about such characters as Davy Crockett, Mike Fink, and Johnny Appleseed to name a few, are a distinctive kind of folk tale that can be considered recent examples of a tradition that dates at least as far back as the Celts.

All folk tales, regardless of their type, are stories that are simultaneously irrational, terrible, and wonderful. They constitute both a literary genre and an experience. When a reader or listener wanders into what John and Caitlin Mathews (1993) call the "perilous land of faery" he or she enters a world of magic, of belief of the whimsical, the fearsome, the triumphant, and the mysterious. The happy ending is perhaps the most significant of the fairy tale traditions providing a sense of justice and solace for the reader. The worthy poor girl of the ashes can indeed become a princess.

Functions of Folk Tales

Folk tales served many social functions in the past but prime among them was that of entertainment. Russian tellers used their entertaining stories to secure food and lodgings, "singing for their supper" for their indulgent hosts. This is evident in the endings which signified the completion of a telling: "There's a tale for you and a crock of butter for me."

Often stories were told to pass the time when tedious manual labor was required to complete a task or the evenings needed to be filled. It was common custom, for instance, for the rural dwellers in southern Georgia around the years 1865–1900 to head down to Shell Point, Florida, each October to purchase a winter's supply of salted fish. Since the trip by wagon took two or three days there was occasion to camp out en route. These evenings were filled with yarn telling around the campfires that were built and word soon spread as to who could tell a good story.

While the basic intent of all stories is to entertain, tales provided a very real mechanism for preserving the cultural inheritance and belief system of a people. The most obvious example of the latter is in myths and legends, often grand and sweeping tales about the origins of the world and how it functions, which are part of every cultural group.

The storytelling session also served the purpose of conveying teachings and understandings about appropriate modes of conduct. Stories have embedded within them the values espoused by a cultural group; what a people should laugh about, despise, revere, desire, and admire. Native American storytellers in storytelling lodges would recite their ancient "wisdom stories" from memory. Upon completion of the telling he or she would say to the listeners, "What did you learn?" And so the question was repeated with each retelling and each new story. The listeners would share their understandings and learn in the process the guiding principles of behavior—respect and tolerance for other's views, due attention to responsibilities within the group, and the acceptance of the consequences of not meeting them. They would also learn that everything in nature has a spirit, and it is the people's role to live in harmony with this spirit.

In addition to being taught the principles by which to live, children were often disciplined with threats about how the gods and ghosts of their folklore would react if their behavior were unacceptable. An example from the Navaho Indians of the Southwestern United States serves as an illustration: Spider Woman was a much revered deity among these ancient peoples, for it was she, they believed, who preserved them in a time when monsters raged on earth. Misbehaving children were told that if their conduct did not improve, Spider Woman would let down her web ladder from her home in Spider Rock and carry them up. Then she would devour them! The sun bleached bones at the top of Spider Rock were those of children who did not behave themselves!

Another function of storytelling, outside of the entertainment and instructional purposes noted above, relates to maintaining the collective psyche or mental health of a people. At the times when many of these tales were broadly told, the peoples understood little of what was happening in the world in which they lived. Norway was overcome in 1351 with the Black Death or bubonic plague that killed two thirds of the population. During this national disaster farmlands decayed and the country went into decline with no one to tend animals and crops. As the people looked for answers, the plague became personified as an old hag who wandered through the parishes of the land with broom and rake. Stories grew up of the sorry encounters people had with the harridan. In this fashion, the tales provided some cold comfort for those suffering.

Similarly, the tales the storyteller told and the songs he sang were one of the few expressions available to the slaves of the American South. Under guise of storytelling a teller could challenge the corrupt and unjust system under which his people were living. The well known trickster tales of Brer Rabbit illustrate this point. While Rabbit is little and seemingly powerless, he manages more often than not to best his bigger opponents, such as Brer Bear, through wit and subterfuge. The analogy to their own situation was not lost on the slaves.

Oral Storytelling Tradition

An ability to tell a story has always been revered for a number of reasons. In earlier times when people had virtually no recourse to print, an individual who became a storyteller took up a role that was both formal and significant in a society. It was the storyteller who preserved the tales, the cultural heritage of the people, by committing them to memory and sharing them with the community. Ted Lewin's delightful picture book, *The Storytellers*, gives some insight into the significance of this role.

But the storyteller was more than a mere mouthpiece or preserver. Tellers recorded historical events such as battles and changing political fortunes of the people in both story and song, thereby becoming oral historians. The activities of the Scandinavian skalds (storytellers) demonstrate how this was done. As a vassal or servant to a noble lord, a skald fought by his master's side and then recounted his lord's glorious deeds or sang of his heroic death after the battle. This very act of keeping and adding to the lore about a people in story meant that the storyteller was developing the cultural character or identity of a societal group.

Quite apart from the social function he was fulfilling, the storyteller/ musician was generally revered for his talents. Prodigious feats of memory were common. A Native American Navajo singer could recite stories about creation that lasted two or three days. Typically the hundreds of songs and stories associated with approximately thirty major ceremonies were known to him. Across the water African griots chanted lengthy genealogies besides telling stories. Similarly the ancient Celtic bards were required to undergo a period of training of about nine years before they were considered fully ready.

Beginnings and Endings and In Between

A storyteller or author, inviting the audience into the land of story, typically uses a formulaic opening that is known to the cultural group being addressed. This greeting signifies that the listener (or the reader) needs to undergo a willing suspension of disbelief and accept the parameters and timelessness of the world about to be described. The most well known of all opening statements to western audiences, of course, is "once upon a time." Sometimes in an oral retelling the listener is required to signify his willingness to participate by joining in a chorus in response to questions asked or statements made by the teller. This is indicated in the African greeting below:

Griot: "A Story—a story."

Listeners: "Let it come, let it go!"

Griot: "Now, what I am going to tell you didn't happen in my part of the forest, but it did happen in a part of the forest far, far away."

Likewise, the Caribbean peoples will use the convention of calling out "Cric" to alert the audience that a story is being offered. If sufficient numbers of people answer "Crac" then the storyteller may begin. Sometimes the call and response will need to be repeated to ensure the will of the group. A particularly amusing call to story is used by the Sewfi storyteller from Ghana:

Storyteller: "Now this story, I didn't make it up!"

Audience: "Who did then?"

The storyteller of the Shangaan people in southeastern Africa is often a woman. She will call out to her people: "Garingani, n'wana wa Garingani," which means, "I am Narrator, daughter of Narrator." The audience will respond with "Garingani! Garingani!" The teller will proceed with her story often clapping her hands, stomping her feet, and singing.

At the end of the tale the listener and/or reader is told when to resume his or her normal frame of mind. This occurs when another formulaic ending or rhyme is uttered, as in the usual western conclusion, "and they all lived happily ever after." Unable to resist a spot of sermonizing, the authors of old would frequently add in a rhyming couplet with some exhortation to behave oneself. French Charles Perrault in his collection of fairy tales published in 1697 was a particular exponent of this art. Likewise, Londoner Richard Johnson, who is credited with publication in 1621 of one of the first adventures of Tom Thumb completed one of the stories about the hero in bawdy fashion:

> *If thou wilt from whipping*
> *keepe safely thy bum,*
> *Take heed of the pastimes,*
> *here taught by Tom Thumbe:*
> *Young Schollers are knauish*
> *and apter to learne*
> *A tricke that's unhappy*
> *then good to discerne*

The stories told by the slaves during the Plantation Era frequently had rhyming phrases both at the beginning and end of the tale. Virginia Hamilton, in her celebration of African-American folk, fairy, and true tales called *Her Stories* uses a number of endings traditional to that group:

So be it,	*Step on a tin,*	*I go around the bend.*
bow bended,	*the tin bends,*	*I see a fence to mend.*
don't you know.	*This is how my story ends.*	*On it is hung my story end.*
My story's ended.		

Sometimes the storytellers of old used a particularly elaborate device to engage their audiences, a device in which they took pride. The *bakhars* and *buffoons* of old Russia used an embellishment called an exordium which is a little story that describes the story but is not connected to the content of the tale. It was generally announced with a flourish and was usually humorous in intent. A typical exordium is noted below:

> *The tale begins with the gray chestnut, with the nag, with the prophetic steed. By the sea, by the ocean, on the island of Buyan, there is a roast bull, beside it is a crushed onion, and three young fellows are going along, they stop and have lunch, and they go on further and start boasting, and they are amusing themselves: we are really brothers at such a place and we eat our fill, more than a peasant woman of dough. This is the exordium, the tale lies before us.*

The ending of the Russian tale is like all endings, a release, often accomplished with an attempt at the same broad humor, spoken fast and rhythmically. Its intent was generally to turn the attention of the listener away from the tale and on to the teller.

> *And I was there, I drank the mead and beer, it flowed over my mustache, but missed my mouth.*

> *This is the story, well, there are no more lies to tell.*

> *Here the tale comes to an end, a fine fellow told it.*

Frequently the *bakhar* drew notice of the audience to himself in hopes of remuneration for the entertainment provided.

> *Here is the tale for you, but for me a string of baked dough rings. For us fine*
> *fellows, a little glass of beer apiece, at the ending of the tale a little wine glass full*
> *of wine.*

Native Americans tended to have different storytelling openings and closing according to tribal affiliation. The storyteller from the Seneca tribe would often begin: "Hanio! Let's have a story!" And end with: "Na-ho! Story's end!"

The plains Cheyenne storyteller would sit in a tipi, touch the bowl of his pipe in ceremonial fashion to the earth, offer a prayer for clarity of speech and begin. The session might last far into the night and the listeners would know it was done when he said: "That cuts it off! Who can tie one on to it?"

Among tribes around the area now known as California the signature ending frequently was abrupt: "And the rat's tail fell off!"

Perhaps one of the most whimsical and idiosyncratic endings has been reported from rural Georgia by Mariella Glenn Hartsfield in her text, *Tall Betsy and Dunce Baby:*

> *I couldn't hang around because I had on paper clothes, and I was afraid the wind*
> *might blow or it might rain. (p. 129)*

The Shangaan Garingani, the woman narrator from southeast Africa who announces in high sprits that she is the daughter of narrator, often spits on the ground in a moment of high drama to ward off evil spirits at the end of the tale.

In order to keep the story going a number of devices are employed by storytellers in almost every culture—transitional phrases, rhyming couplets, repetition of nonsense syllables, or songs. These, of course, tended to be idiosyncratic to the teller but a number of these ploys were and still are recognizable across cultural groups. For example, Russian storytellers used the phrase or a variation of it, "Do not grieve, lie down and sleep, morning is wiser than evening." a number of times across the life of a tale as a way of keeping the adventure moving. Similarly in some Native American societies the teller will ask, "Are you listening?" The nature of the audience response will or will not confirm this!

When the transitional statement is a refrain that is either sung or chanted every so often, the story is called a cante fable or a prose narrative with verse. This is a common structure in black folk tales of the south. Occasionally these chants are heightened with nonsense syllables that are difficult to translate. Hamilton's retelling of a Creole tale called *Marie and the Redfish* in *Her Stories* complete with the chants serves as a fine example. When Marie wants to talk to her lover who has been made into a fish she cries out:

Caliwa wa, caliwa, co.

Waco, Mother says yes (Maman dit oui).

Waco, Father says no (Papa dit non).

Caliwa wa, caliwaco.

Typically these formulaic verbal rituals that accompanied a storytelling are not reproduced in a tale that has been committed to print either in picture book or illustrated book format. The role of the story as teacher is also made explicit in the formulaic beginnings and endings of tales used by a teller. The traditional beginning of an Ashanti tale: "We do not really mean, we do not really mean, that what we are going to say is true," suggests that always there is a grain of truth, a kernel of wisdom, a lesson to be learned. Likewise, the Sudanese convey this subtle and complex understanding in the following formula associated with their storytelling:

Teller: "I'm going to tell a story."
Audience: "Right!"
Teller: "It's a lie."
Audience: "Right!"
Teller: "But not everything in it is false."
Audience: "Right!"

After the story is delivered the experience ends very satisfactorily when the teller announces:

"I put the tale back where I found it."

It is not possible to identify all beginnings and endings of stories that have been used by various cultural groups. Listed below are some according to country or ethnic group that have been identified in texts.

Beginnings:

American, (Appalachia)

Once upon a time, not my time, not your time, but once upon a time . . .
(McCarthy, 1994, p. 180)

Back in the old times . . .
(Chase, 1943/1971, p. 151)

American (Creek)

The old-time beings were gathered together . . .
(Lankford, 1987, p. 118)

American Cajun)

Back in the old country . . .
(Reneaux, 1992, p. 95)

Australian
   In the beginning all was darkness forever . . .
            (Hamilton, 1988, p. 47)

Celtic
   In the days when music was sweeter and fire was hotter and ice was colder
and drink was stronger than it is now . . .
            (Williamson, 1991, p. 88)

Egyptian
   This happened, or maybe it did not. The time is long past, and much is
forgotten . . .
            (Bushnaq, 1986, p. 89)

German
   Once upon a time in the middle of winter when snowflakes were falling
from the sky like feathers . . .
            (Thompson, 1968, p. 326)

Hmong
   Many, many New Year's festivals ago . . .
            (Livo & Cha, 1991, p. 64)

Iraqi
   In the days when the streams flowed in the wadis and breezes blew on
the hills, when gray-haired women huddled together and gossiped, in those
days . . .
            (Bushnaq, 1986, p. 348)

Irish
   More years ago than you can tell me, and twice as many as I can tell you . . .
            (Sawyer, 1942/1970, p. 239)

Italian
   Long, long ago as far back as the time when animals spoke . . .
            (deCaro, 1992, p. 73)

   It was the custom in a certain village . . .
            (Calvino, 1956/1981, p. 133)

Japanese
   Very, very long ago in a certain place there . . .
            (Cole, 1982, p. 519)

Russian
   In olden days in a certain kingdom, not in our land . . .
            (Afanas'ev, 1973, p. 545)

Scottish
   Once upon a time when all big folk were wee ones and all likes were true . . .
            (Cole, 1982, p. 281)

Siberian
> My story had its start a long, long time ago when the earth was young . . .
> > (Riordan, 1989, p. 88)

Endings:

Appalachian
> Last time I was down there they were all gettin' on right well.
> > (Chase, 1943/1971, p. 88)

Celtic
> So it ends.
> > (Williamson, 1991, p. 49)

German
> Grief came to an end and joy began.
> > (Grimm & Grimm, 1944/1972, p. 271)

> Open the windows that the lies may fly out.
> > (Grimm & Grimm, 1944/1972, p. 662)

Iraqi
> So they all lived a happy and comfortable life. May it be so for every husband and wife. . .
> > (Bushnaq, 1986, p. 150)

Irish
> This is a true story. They are all lies but this one.
> > (Colum, 1992, p. 495)

Japanese
> His descendants flourished too, or so they say.
> > (Williston, ca 1910, p. 250)

Norse
> Snip, snap, snover; this tale is over.
> > (Thompson, 1968, p. 187)

Russian
> There's a tale for you and a crock of butter for me.
> > (Husain, 1994, p. 173)

Siberian
> Happy and more than a whit wiser.
> > (Riordan, 1989, p. 123)

Syrian
> After which they lived in happiness and bliss,
> With plenty of sons and daughters to kiss,
> May God grant each of us joy such as this.
> > (Bushnaq, 1986, p. 205)

Texts Cited

Afanas'ev, A. (1973). *Russian Fairy Tales*. New York: Pantheon Books.

Bushnaq, I. (Translator & Ed.) (1986). *Arab Folktales*. New York: Pantheon Books.

Caduto, M. J. & J. Bruchac. (1989). *Keepers of the Earth*. Illustrated by John Kahionhes Fadden and Carol Wood. Golden, Colorado: Fulcrum, Inc.

Calvino, I. (Ed.) (1956/1981). *Italian Folktales*. New York: Pantheon Books.

Chase, R. (Collector). (1943/1971). *The Jack Tales*. Boston: Houghton Mifflin.

Cole, J. (Ed.) (1982). *Best-Loved Folktales of the World*. New York: Doubleday.

Colum, P. (Ed). (1992). *Treasury of Irish Folklore*. New York: Wings Books.

Grimm, J. & Grimm, W. (1944/1972, Hunt, M., Translator). *The Complete Grimm's Fairy Tales*. New York: Pantheon Books.

DeCaro, F. (Ed.) (1992). *The Folktale Cat*. Little Rock, AR: August House.

Hamilton, V. (1995). *Her Stories*. Illustrated by Leo & Diane Dillon. New York: The Blue Sky Press.

Hamilton, V. (1988). *In the Beginning*. New York: Alfred A. Knopf.

Hartsfield, M. G. (1991). *Tall Betsy and Dunce Baby*. Athens: University of Georgia Press.

Husain, S. (1994). *Daughters of the Moon*. Winchester, MA: Faber & Faber.

Kipling, R. (1978). *Just So Stories*. New York: Weathervane Books.

Lankford, G. E. (Ed.) *Native American Legends*. Little Rock, AR: August House.

Lewin, T. (1998). *The Storytellers*. Illustrated by the author. New York: Lothrop, Lee & Shepard Books.

Livo, N. & Cha, D. (Eds.) (1991). *Folk Stories of the Hmong*. Englewood, CO: Libraries Unlimited.

Mathews, J & Mathews, C. (1993). *The Fairy Tale Reader*. San Francisco: HarperCollins Publishers.

McCarthy, W. (Ed.) (1994). *Jack in Two Worlds*. Chapel Hill: University of North Carolina Press.

Milord, S. (1996). *Tales of the Shimmering Sky*. Illustrated by JoAnne E. Kitchel. Charlotte, Vermont: Williamson Publishing.

Reneaux, J. J. (1992). *Cajun Folktales*. Little Rock, AR: August House.

Riordan, J. (Collector & Translator). (1986). *Sun Maiden and the Crescent Moon*. New York: Interlink Books

Savory, P. (1988). *The Best of African Folklore*. Illustrated by Gina Daniel. Cape Town: Struuik Timmins.

Sawyer, R. (1942/1970). *The Way of the Storyteller*. New York: Penguin Books.

Thompson, S. (E.). (1968). *One Hundred Favorite Folktales*. Bloomington: Indiana University Press.

Tyler, R. (Ed.) (1987). *Japanese Tales*. New York: Pantheon Books.

Williamson, R. (Collector). (1991). *Wise and Foolish Tongue*. San Francisco, CA: Chronicle Books.

2

Western Myths
and Legends

What is a Myth?

Myths are stories that arose and evolved in ancient societies. They were told in the absence of scientific information to explain the workings of the world—the rising and setting of the sun, the clapping of thunder, flooding, drought, and volcanic eruptions. Often these attempts to understand the inexplicable required invoking deities such as gods. So to some extent myths are stories about the relationship of higher beings with each other and with man.

The fact that myths exist at all presupposes that humans became aware of themselves as spiritual beings. Since myths are essentially religious in nature they should be treated with respect. This is sometimes difficult for the contemporary mind to do as the stories appear quaint, lewd, bawdy, irrational, and straight out bizarre in light of current understandings and beliefs. It is for this reason the word mythical has come to be equated with incredible in the English language. For instance, it is hard for modern people to accept most creation stories. In one example, David A. Anderson has retold a myth of the Yoruba people, a large cultural group in the west of Africa, and named it *The Origins of Life on Earth*. According to this myth the supreme god, Olorun, gave permission to his messenger Obatala to create earth and all that is upon it, including man. Obatala does so but in the process loses the egg he is carrying which contains all the personalities from the sky kingdom. It cracks and the contents scatter. This accounts for the variability of life today.

Accounting for the variability of life and the tensions and adventures that arise when creatures of different natures coexist is an interesting subject of myth in many cultures. Generally the opposing forces are personified in some way. Evil is often portrayed as a hag, a witch, a snake, or in beings who cannot die. One such figure is Koschei the Deathless, a powerful being in Russian folk tales who is thought to be immortal as he is not bound by the ordinary laws of existence. His heart, which is his only vulnerable organ, is outside of his body and opponents can be free of Koschei's venom only if they can determine its location.

The nature of the myths depends in some measure upon the climatic conditions under which the societal group who devised them was living. According to the Norse, human beings arose from the licking of frozen stones by a divine cow name Audumla. The after world these human beings descended to was a bare, misty, featureless plain haunted by shivering, starving ghosts. The Greeks, with their kinder climate, attributed the development of human beings to the titan, or elder god, Prometheus. On a flowery river bank he kneaded people statues from mud which the goddess Athena subsequently brought to life. Most Greek ghosts or shades went to everlasting torment in an underground cavern, bereft of flowers and sunshine and ruled by the unlovely god, Hades. Great and virtuous Greeks, or those favored by the gods, went to a place of contentment, immortality, and light, considered blessed, called the Elysian Fields on the western margin of the earth.

While most myths are considered the creation of minds seeking rationality in a seemingly irrational world, there is occasionally evidence that supports the claims of a story or coincides with scientific understanding. Archaeological excavations on the island of Crete have revealed the existence of the labyrinth spoken of in Greek tales. The most well known story of this maze involves King Minos and the Minotaur.

Myths in their purest forms have not traditionally been the subjects of books for children. Perhaps this is because the subject matter is often very violent, frequently prurient, or overtly sexual and not considered appropriate fare for young readers. As an example, King Minos failed to fulfill a pledge he had made to the sea god, Poseidon, to sacrifice a bull. The deity imposed a terrible revenge. He ensured that Minos' consort, Pasiphae, became sexually infatuated with the beast and eventually gave birth to the hybrid monster known as the Minotaur, the bull of Minos. Such information is carefully and appropriately (given the target audience of most picture books), overlooked by Warwick Hutton in his retelling and illustrating of the picture book, *Theseus and the Minotaur.*

What is a Legend?

Legend comes from the Latin, *legenda*, meaning "things to be read." Legends, sometimes called hero tales, have as their intent the recounting of courageous deeds of mortals who are frequently at odds with the gods, monsters, nature, or simply themselves. In the original sense of the word, legends applied to stories about Christian saints as figures to be admired or emulated but are now considered to be accounts of the exploits of both real and imaginary people.

It is not always easy to distinguish between legend and historical fact. The romantic English King Arthur is a case in point. This royal, whose battles with men and beasts are legion, whose table was round and whose knights were gallant, is a somewhat shadowy historical figure. While it is generally believed that such a warrior chief existed, he did not attain the stature awarded him in the legends.

As it is no simple matter to distinguish between legend and fact, it is not always easy to distinguish between myths and legends. For example, Saint Patrick, the patron saint of Ireland was a real person and some details of his life are known. There are many stories attributed to the good saint, some of which are believable and others which, while good tales, require the willing suspension of disbelief. It is within the bounds of credibility that Patrick used the three leafed shamrock to illustrate the holy trinity. It is not within the limits of believability to think that Patrick and his followers escaped the wrath of the pagan king, Laoghaire, by changing themselves into deer and running in the forest. The ability to take on the shape of any living creature is more closely associated with mythology than legend.

The people of the past took the passing down of sacred myths and legends seriously and wished for them to be related in as true a fashion as possible. For this reason only certain people within many Native American tribes were allowed to tell them. W. B. Yeats (1888) a noted collector of Irish folklore, reports that Irish storytellers would sit together in the evening and tell a given legend. They would then vote on the "correct" version and anyone whose telling varied had to reconcile his version. Thus tales were handed down with accuracy over the ages. The long Celtic story of *Diedre* is an example of one such story whose sacredness was guarded in such a fashion. How closely the story adheres to the original cannot be known, but there is available an illustrated version of this story by David Guard (1977).

Like myths, many of the legends that are now appearing in print, particularly in picture book and illustrated book form where the reading audience is likely to be children, have been tempered to meet modern sensibilities. The African story about an old woman who irritated the god, Onyankopon, with her incessant chatting and inadvertent beating of him is illustrative. In a traditional version Onyankopon took leave of his earthly dwelling and returned to the heavens to escape the daily haranguing. The distraught woman built a tower so that she could continue her dialogue with the god. But she was one mortar short in attaining this goal. In a traditional telling she seeks this mortar from the bottom of the tower. This causes the edifice to fall, killing many people. Ruby Dee (1991) has modified this ending in her picture book version called *A Tower to Heaven*, such that the people do not die but are instead continually replacing the top mortar with the bottom. The irrepressible protagonist, Yaa, continues to call out to Onyankopon and every so often can be heard shouting, "One more mortar."

The Greek and Roman Tradition

The myths and legends of ancient Greece are a rich bequest to western civilization. Literature, psychology, and common conversation are replete with references to the gods, figures, and heroes featured in these stories. Romans were the first to embrace and enhance the religion and science of the Greeks. With one or two exceptions, such as Janus the god of doorways and beginnings, the Roman gods were also those of the Greeks. See figure 1 for a listing of the names of the deities used in the respective cultures and their areas of interest.

In contrast to the myths of other societies that preceded them, the Greeks entertained gods in the likeness of themselves. Not for these ancients were the half-people, half-animal images of the Egyptians or the bestial beasts of the Mesopotamians. Unlike these earlier civilizations, the Greeks chose to worship the beauty of the human body. The gods Apollo and Hermes were portrayed as young men who were at an age of great physical beauty. Likewise, Greek heroes were beautiful to gaze upon. Hercules was reputed to be the strongest man in the world and carried himself with the supreme confidence that comes with such knowledge.

In addition, the activities of the gods of the Greeks are in many ways reassuringly familiar. They ate, drank, carried on questionable dalliances, and amused themselves just as people do. Their world was a humanized one. Furthermore, citizens could tell you where some of their gods and heroes resided. Despite having to wander and to do battle with monsters for much of his life, Hercules was said to have had a home in the city of Thebes. Any ancient could have explained that off the shore of the island of Cythera was where Aphrodite, the goddess of love and beauty, was born in the foam. Persephone, wife of the god of the underworld, Hades, lived on the island of Sicily as did the unfortunate Scylla. The latter was a sea nymph who unwillingly incurred the wrath of a sorceress, *Circe*, who turned her into a monster and finally a rock on the Sicilian coast.

But while most Greek gods bear good will toward people and can be propitiated and manipulated, they are to be respected for they will not be deceived or denied. If this occurs they exact an angry vengeance with their superhuman powers. Apollo, the lyre playing god, turned the feathers of the raven black. He did this after the then white bird brought a message that the comely Coronis favored a mortal over the god himself. The luckless, or perhaps foolish, Coronis was killed. It is the gods alone who have the final word in social intercourse with their supreme gift and privilege of immortality.

Figure 1. Greek and Roman Pantheon

The Major Gods			Other Important Deities		
Greek	Roman	Concern	Greek	Roman	Concern
Zeus	Jupiter	sky	Hestia	Vesta	hearth
Hera	Juno	marriage	Hellios	Sol	sun
Poseidon	Neptune	sea	Selene	Luna	moon
Demeter	Ceres	corn	Eros	Amor	love
Apollon	Apollo	law	Pan	Pan	flocks
Artemis	Diana	hunting	Persephone	Prosperina	springtime
Hermes	Mercury	commerce	Hades	Pluto	underworld
Athene	Minerva	learning			
Hephaistos	Vulcan	handicrafts			
Aphrodite	Venus	procreation			
Ares	Mars	war			
Dionysus	Bacchus	wine			

Beside this special privilege of everlasting life most members of the pantheon of the gods lived in considerable splendor on Olympus, which was thought to be the center of the world. Olympus was considered to be both a mountain, Greece's highest in the northeast of the country, and a mysterious place or region above the mountains. Wherever it was, the entrance was a gate of clouds kept by the seasons. Beyond the gate, the dwellings of the gods were placed in a setting where no wind blew, where no rain fell, and ambrosia or nectar was the food eaten. Each god was responsible for and had dominion over a piece of the universe.

Greek and Roman stories represented a revolution in thought since they placed humans at the center of the universe for the first time. In the tales of most other previous cultures, animals were heavily featured and considered to be equal, if not superior, to men in the order of things. These stories, some of which are described below, have fascinated man for centuries.

Classical Myths and Legends
The Trojan War

One of the most famous cities of the ancient world, Troy, was situated in the eastern end of the Mediterranean. It remains a spot of some repute because of the battles that were fought there over the treachery of a woman. Helen, the fairest of her sex in all the world, was married to Menelaus. In her husband's absence she was wooed by Paris, son of King Priam of Troy. The lovers fled to the protection of that walled city. Menelaus gathered together a large army of Helen's former suitors who had sworn an oath to bring back his wife and to avenge his betrayal. One of the commanders expected to respond to the request for retribution was Odysseus (Ulysses in Latin), King of the island of Ithaca. Odysseus viewed the lust for revenge as romantic folly and feigned madness when a messenger came to summon him. Alas, he was outwitted. So it was that Odysseus left his young wife, the fair Penelope, and their three year old son and set off as a commander within the great fleet of 1,000 ships to the strong and fortified city of Troy.

For 10 years the Trojans and the Greeks battled, neither able to gain advantage. Over time the war took a toll on all participants and the gods of Olympus who were ranged against one another. Ares, the god of war was on the side of the Trojans; while Poseidon, god of the sea, favored the Greeks. Finally, it became apparent that the conflict could not be resolved since the strong walls of the city repudiated all sieges and insults. The town, well fortified, remained strong.

It was the wily Odysseus who hatched the plot to gain advantage over the Trojans by employing the element of surprise. The Greeks decided to build a large wooden horse into which would be secreted a number of men, Odysseus among them. After the beast was fashioned, the men took up posts within and the Greek army retreated as though finally conceding the hopelessness of the situation. But the ships had merely removed themselves from view and were prepared to sail back to assist their fellows in the horse when it was taken into the city. The odd offering was dragged in the gates by the hapless Trojans and left at the temple of the goddess, Athena. In the night the chieftains emerged from the belly of the horse, opened the gates of the city, and let in the returning army. Buoyed by their audacity and with surprise, the Greeks were able to vanquish their enemies of 10 years.

Poseiden, the Lord of the Sea and a staunch advocate for the Greeks, was distressed after the battle since the victors forgot to pay him due respect. His anger turned him from ally to enemy and punishment became Poseiden's driving desire. As a result many of the Greek warriors lost their lives in the waves and storms on their homeward journey. Odysseus did not but he was to suffer for 10 more long years, essentially a captive of the sea, before he was to return to his family. Fortunately for the student of classic myth and legend, there are many stories about the continuing trials of the trickster Odysseus.

Picture Books and Illustrated Texts: The Trojan War
Connolly, Peter. (1992). *The Legend of Odysseus*. Illustrated by the author. Oxford: Oxford University Press. Peter Connolly has provided a highly readable account of the events relayed above. Of considerable interest to the reader are the historical notes relating to costume and armor, archeological findings, sea routes, and more.

Fisher, Leonard Everett. (1991). *Cyclops*. Illustrated by the author. New York: Holiday House. On the way home from the Trojan War, Odysseus and his Greek army land on an island. Tired and hungry the men seek refuge in a cave well stocked with milk, cheese, and meat. It is the home of the malevolent giant Cyclops, Polyphemus. He traps the visitors, devours two for his evening meal, and proceeds to eat two more men for breakfast the next day. With cunning, Odysseus then outwits Polyphemus making him the laughing stock of his kind.

Hutton, Warwick. (1992). *The Trojan Horse*. Illustrated by the author. New York: Margaret K. McElderry Books. Hutton retells in compelling fashion the ancient and tragic story of the Trojan horse. The author's watercolors are poignant and evocative.

Little, Emily. (1988). *The Trojan Horse*. Illustrated by Michael Eagle. New York: Random House. This simplified version of the Trojan Wars details the fortress at Troy, explaining how difficult it was to breach and describes the arrival of the Greeks, the protracted war effort, the building of the wooden horse, and the fall of Troy. A little history is provided the reader as to how the story has come down in time through the writings of Homer.

Theseus and the Minotaur

Minos, the powerful ruler of Crete, lost his only son when the boy was on a foolish and dangerous errand for the Athenian king—trying to kill a bull. In his anger Minos attacked the city of Athens and declared he would raze it unless every seven years (or by some accounts, nine years), a tribute of seven maidens and seven youths were sent to sustain his minotaur (half-man, half-bull). The monster was captive deep in a vast labyrinth. When he is of age, Theseus, the son of Aegeus, the king of Athens, elects to go in place of one of the men to try to put an end to this killing. With the help of Ariadne, the daughter of the king of Crete, Theseus is able to find the minotaur in his labyrinth and to slay him after a battle. Unfortunately, the return home of the Athenians is marred by two events—Theseus' mistreatment of Ariadne and the death of his father, Aegeus. The old man was never to see the white sail on the returning ship which signified the successful slaying of the minotaur.

The designer of the labyrinth in which the minotaur was contained was Daedelus, and it was he who showed Ariadne how Theseus could escape from the maze. When King Minos deduced that fact, he was angry. In his fury, the ruler imprisoned both the architect and his son, Icarus, in the labyrinth reasoning that the man who designed it would know there was no escape. But Daedelus was not known to be clever and resourceful for nothing. He and his son escaped their prison but the price was high. Jane Yolen has a moving version of this story.

Picture Books: Theseus and the Minotaur

Hutton, Warwick. (1989). *Theseus and the Minotaur*. Illustrated by the author. New York: Margaret K. McElderry Books. Ariadne, the daughter of the king of Crete, who betrays her father is featured in this story of the death of the minotaur at the hands of Theseus, but her role tends to be underplayed by Hutton. Most of the glory goes to the brave prince. As in the traditional versions, the return home of the Athenians is marred by the death of Theseus' father.

Orgel, Doris. (1994). *Ariadne Awake*. Illustrated by Barry Moser. New York: Viking. *Ariadne Awake* is the story of the slaying of the monster told from the perspective of the daughter of the king of Crete. In picturesque language, Orgel relays how Ariadne chooses to go against her father, how she comes to fall in love with Theseus at personal cost, and how she is betrayed. Ariadne eventually finds happiness in a marriage with the god, Dionysus. An epilogue is used by the author to speculate on Theseus' motives.

Yolen, Jane. (1991). *Wings*. Illustrated by Dennis Nolan. Orlando, Florida: Harcourt Brace Jovanovich, Publishers. Yolen's retelling of the famed story of how the clever Daedalus is punished by the gods for his overweening pride could match any previous versions of this oft told tale. Included in the punishment, of course, is the loss of his bright eyed son, Icarus, who flies too close to the sun. Nolan's illustrations are majestic and add considerably to the power of the retelling.

The Story of Persephone

One of the more tragic figures in Greek mythology is Persephone, or Prosperine in Latin. She ruled the vague, shadowy underworld with the god Hades, a world that goes by his name. But the girl was not a willing partner in this world of ghosts, sometimes known as shades. Persephone is the much loved daughter of the goddess of all growing things, Demeter. One day when Persephone in company with nymphs is looking at some beautiful narcissi flowers, Hades springs out from a chasm in a chariot and carries her away to be his bride. Filled with grief, Demeter refuses to let the earth live and it turns dry and frozen. Zeus, the head god, is forced to intervene in this struggle between the two lesser gods to save the world from famine. He rules that because Persephone had absently eaten four small pomegranate seeds during her captivity, she is doomed to four months of each year in the underworld. She can return to her mother for the other months of the year. The return of flowers in spring each year signals that Demeter and her daughter are again reunited.

Picture Books: Persephone

Hutton, Warwick. (1994). *Persephone*. Illustrated by the author. New York: Margaret K. McElderry Books. This version of *Persephone*, the ancient Greek story of winter and summer, is parallel to the explanation offered above. Hutton has managed to complement his telling with lovely water colors that take up the mood of the individual seasons.

Birrer, Cynthia and William. (1987). *Song to Demeter*. Illustrated by the authors. New York: Lothrop, Lee & Shepard Books. The Birrers have chosen a mixture of Greek and Roman deities in their retelling of the story of the seasons. Demeter, is called by her Greek name of Persephone; but in this iteration it is Pluto, the Roman god of the dead, who carries off Persephone to live in the darkness of Hades. Pluto is also named as Demeter's brother. What distinguishes this telling is the unusual illustrations, machine stitched appliqué and embroidery on fabric; they have a significant depth of color and abandon to them.

King Midas' Story
Midas was a legendary king of a land called Phrygia. He performed an act of kindness that was to have amazing consequences. He did not know that the old, lost man, Silenus, brought to him by peasants was the foster father of the god of wine, Bacchus. Bacchus was gratified by the king's kindly hospitality and offered a reward of his own naming. The foolish royal was soon to sorely regret his request that everything he touched would turn to gold. While he delighted in turning leaves and stone to gold, he was horrified when his food also changed into the bright metal. No sooner had King Midas put his lips to bread than it hardened as did the wine he drank and the meat he touched. The king, facing starvation, began to see his wish as an affliction. Frantically Midas beseeched Bacchus for help. The deity relented telling the king to go to the fountainhead of the River Pactolus and plunge his head and body in. The waters would wash away his gift and curse. When Midas followed the god's directions, the sands of the river took up the gold and remain so colored today. (It was mined up until the time of the Roman Augustus.) Today, of course, the expression a Midas touch, means an individual who is seemingly successful in all commercial enterprises.

Picture Book: King Midas' Story
Hawthorne. Nathaniel. (1987). *King Midas and the Golden Touch*. Retold and illustrated by Kathryn Hewitt. San Diego: Harcourt Brace Jovanovich, Publishers. Kathryn Hewitt's version omits the reference to Bacchus. Instead the king is approached by a spirit while he is counting his gold in his basement and offers him an unlimited supply. It was, of course, too good to be true. When his beloved daughter was turned to gold, Midas realized the error he had made and begged the spirit for the enchantment to be reversed.

While King Midas' story seems to have a happy ending here, the king was not long blessed. Eschewing the wealth and splendor he had so ardently sought, Midas went to live in the country. Subsequently he became entangled with the pipe-playing, goat-footed, horned god Pan of the flocks. When Apollo heard Midas praising Pan's musical talents over his own ability to play the lyre, he grew angry. The god of law and justice turned the king's ears into those of a jackass. Midas covered up his shame and the long floppy ears with a hat for a time but eventually had to have a hair cut. The barber swore an oath that he would tell no one of the king's secret. He was true to his word— in a fashion. While he told no person, he dug a hole deep in the country and shouted the peculiar news into it and felt relief! But the words sprouted in the ground and grew in the reeds. When the wind blows them about, a listener can hear in the rustling, "Midas has jackass ears!" A telling of this story is to be found in a text by Mordicai Gerstein called *Tales of Pan*.

The Story of Pygmalion

The story of Pygmalion was told only by the Romans and so the goddess of love who is featured in the retellings is the Roman god, Venus. Despite this, the story is closely associated with Cyprus which was part of the Greek states in the ancient world.

Pygmalion is an artist, a gifted and handsome artist, who is much sought after by the ladies. He is also a misogynist and he spurns all unsought affections. But the fairer sex is to have revenge. Pygmalion carves a statue of a woman who is so beautiful and so life like that the artist falls in love with her. The man is then obsessed with his creation, bringing the lifeless maiden fine and charming gifts as would a lover. Finally, on the day of the feast of Venus, a festival especially honored in Cyprus, Pygmalion could bear it no longer. At the temple he prayed that he would find a woman like the statue at home. As much as he wanted, he did not dare ask for the life of the marble woman he thought of as Galatea. But Venus knew Pygmalion's secret desire and the passion attendant on the desire . She was intrigued also by the oddity of a man in love with a statue and granted him his wish. Not much is known about the married life of Pygmalion and Galatea except that in time they bore a son, Paphos.

Picture Books: Pygmalion

Espeland, Pamela. (1981). *The Story of Pygmalion*. Illustrated by Catherine Cleary. Minneapolis: Carolrhoda Books, Inc. The story told by Espeland is faithful to the classic version of the tale. What makes this iteration of the story a delight are the illustrations. Throughout the images of the classic Greek architecture and dress are pictures of cats in various poses, spilled wine, pet birds, and riotous plants. The bright colors add to the festive feeling that is present throughout the story despite Pygmalion's initial despair at his situation.

Atalanta's Story

Atalanta was a maiden of great beauty and awe inspiring physical prowess. She had, for example, wounded the boar sent to ravage the land and cattle of King Oeneus by the goddess Artemis.

Atalanta's amazing physical strengths grew from her childhood. Abandoned on a mountainside by her father at birth, her care was taken on initially by a she-bear. Some hunters then took up the responsibility providing Atlanta with opportunity to learn and subsequently thrive with a bow and arrow. Perhaps her most well known story is that of the race she undergoes at the request of her now reconciled father to decide a marriage partner. The accounts of this race differ slightly in the versions below.

Picture Books: Atalanta's Race

Climo, Shirley. (1995). *Atalanta's Race*. Illustrated by Alexander Koshkin. New York: Clarion Books. Atalanta's fame, derived from her physical feats in contests, spread to the now aging and lonely King Iasus. He recognizes and claims the girl as his own. Still without a male heir, Iasus urges Atalanta to marry. She agrees only to wed the suitor who could outrun her. This honor went to Melanion, simply because he had the assistance of Aphrodite, the goddess of love. But because the pair never thank her, the goddess turned them into a lioness and lion, to run forever.

Martin, Claire. (1991). *The Race of the Golden Apples*. Illustrated by Leo and Diane Dillon. New York: Dial Books for Young Readers. Diana, the Goddess of the Hunt, along with Crona, the she-bear, protect and nurture the infant Atalanta in the woods. The child grows into a handsome woman with a heart hardened by the news that her father is the violent King Iasus. Nonetheless, Atalanta agrees to go and live with the now aging, regretful ruler. Her resolve not to marry cannot be broken by the line of suitors until she meets Hippomenes. With the help of Venus and three magic apples, Hippomenes is able to claim the girl of the forest. The Dillon's illustrations in blues and greens are stunning.

Cupid and Psyche

Cupid is the Roman god of love known as Eros in Greek. One tradition makes Eros the child of the goddess Aphrodite and her lover, Ares, the god of War. Once a handsome young man, Cupid is often depicted now as a round cherub bearing a bow from which he shoots arrows of love and desire.

Psyche is a mere mortal but one of unsurpasing beauty who inadvertently incurs the wrath of Venus. The goddess calls upon her mischievous son, Cupid, to use his magical arrows to make the girl fall in love with a frightening creature. By a twist of fate it is Cupid himself who is nicked by the arrow, and he is greatly smitten by the lovely girl. Psyche then goes to live on a mountain with Cupid; but the creature of the gods while kind beyond measure, refuses to let his love view him. Overcome by curiosity, Psyche finally gazes upon Cupid while he sleeps. He is then lost to her. To win him back, Psyche has to perform three impossible tasks set by the vengeful Venus. The girl is aided in her performance of these dangerous, onerous deeds by the still love struck Cupid. Once completed, the three tasks break the spell of Venus upon her son and he is now free to become fully a husband to Psyche, a match blessed by the greatest Roman god himself, Jupiter. As with most classic tales the versions below differ slightly.

Picture Books: Cupid and Psyche

Craft, M. Charlotte. (1996). *Cupid and Psyche*. Illustrated by K.Y. Craft. New York: Morrow Junior Books. Despite or perhaps because of her great beauty Psyche is lonely, as suitors dare not approach her. When she does capture the god, Cupid, and becomes his wife, it is her sisters who spoil her happiness. Psyche, however, overcomes her siblings jealousy and in time is able to take her place as a goddess with her husband. This age-old tale, similar in theme to Beauty and the Beast, is brought fully to life in this lovely telling.

Hodges, Margaret. (1989). *The Arrow and the Lamp*. Illustrated by Donna Diamond. Boston: Little, Brown and Company. Psyche is enamored of a Greek god called Eros in this tale. Hodges is a deft storyteller and does the story justice in her long picture book. Likewise, Diamond's illustrations are both sweeping and poignant.

Hercules' Story

Hercules was the hero most admired in all of Greece. He was the strongest of men and, short of magic, no physical task could defeat him. He was not an intellectual hero; but he certainly was an emotional one, and it was this latter characteristic that was his undoing. Hercules spent much of his life atoning for one rash deed after another. This humility and willingness to pay penance endeared him to the people and was the reason he was considered great.

Hercules had a distinguished but cursed parentage. His father was Zeus and his mother was Alcmena, a mortal and an unwitting partner to the god. Hera, Zeus's spiteful and jealous wife, took out her fury many times on her husband's offspring. Her first attempt to kill Hercules was made when he was a mere baby. She sent two snakes into the nursery. As they flicked their tongues, reared, and coiled themselves around the child, he merely laughed and twisted them to death. Such an act was a precursor to a reckless life.

The education of Hercules as a child was attended to with great care. While the hero excelled at sports and athletic endeavors, his interest in music, considered a significant part of the training of a Greek, was minimal. One day in anger he rebelled against his teacher and inadvertently killed him. While filled with deepest remorse, there were no lessons learned. Later on he killed his beloved wife, the Princess Megara, along with their three sons. Hercules was to bear this burden of sorrow for the rest of his life, even though the savagery was at the instigation of the ever present and ever deceitful Hera. He was insane at the time of the murder.

The suffering hero offered himself as a slave to a crafty king, Eurystheus of Mycenae, at the urging of the oracle of Delphi as a means of making amends for his terrible behavior. Urged by Hera the king devised a series of tasks for the penitent without equal in their demands. Frequently these tasks are known as the labors of Hercules and they are listed below.

1. The Lion of Nemea: The lion of the island of Nemea was monstrous. No weapon had ever pierced its hide, so Heracles beat and choked it. He skinned the beast and wore the hide as a protective garment with the head as a hood.

2. The Lernean Hydra: The serpent of the swamp in Lernea had nine heads that doubled each time they were cut off. Hercules secured the assistance of his nephew, Iolaus. The boy cauterized each head as Hercules struck them so no more could grow and the one immortal head left at the end of the adventure was buried under a rock.

3. The Cerynean Hind: A stage with horns of gold and hooves of bronze was to be brought back alive to the mean spirited king. As it was an animal sacred to the goddess Artemis, the beast could not be harmed. It took Hercules a year to hunt it down.

4. The Erymanthian Boar: A great boar living on the slopes of Mount Erymanthus was laying waste to the area. Hercules captured the beast by chasing it to exhaustion. When he brought the boar back to Eurysthesus, the king was so frightened he hid in a huge urn.

5. The Augean Stables: Augeas, the son of Helios the sun god, kept thousands of cattle in stables that had not been cleaned for years and they were piled high with dung. Hercules had one day to clean them out. He did so by the device of diverting two rivers, Alpheus and Peneus, through the stables.

6. The Stymphalian Birds: Lake Stymphalos was infested with huge numbers of man-eating birds. Hercules cleared the birds by scaring them out of the trees with castanets and then shooting them one by one with his bow and arrow.

7. The Cretan Bull: Poseidon, the god of the sea, had given King Minos a beautiful, savage bull. Hercules was ordered to go to Crete and capture this wild, fire-breathing animal which he brought back to Eurystheus.

8. The Mares of Diomedes: In the city of Thrace lived a herd of mares owned by a king Diomedes, who fed them with the flesh of strangers. Hercules first killed the king, fed the mares his flesh, and then took the animals back to his master.

9. The Girdle of Hippolyte: Hera was up to her mischief in the ninth labor. Hercules was asked to bring back the beautiful girdle that belonged to Hippolyte, the Queen of the Amazons. Hippolyte was willing but Hera stirred up the people, making them believe that Hercules was going to

carry off their leader. The Amazons charged down the ship; Hercules was forced to kill Hippolyte.

10. The Cattle of Geryon: To reach these red cattle that were guarded by a three headed monster, Hercules had to travel to an island beyond Spain. This venture involved a lot of killing; Geryon, the monster, his giant herdsman, and the two-headed watch dog called Orthus were all slain. During this labor the hero sailed through the Straits of Gibraltar and set up the twin Pillars of Hercules on either side.

11. The Apples of the Hesperides: This was the most difficult of all the labors since it involved Hercules using his wits. The Hesperides who, guarded by the golden apples, were the daughters of Atlas, the titan holding up the world. Hercules went to Atlas and offered to hold up the world if Atlas would get the apples for him. Atlas, seeing a chance to rid himself of his tiresome burden forever offered to take the fruit to Erystheus, himself. Hercules agreed, only if the titan would take the sky for a moment while he placed a pad on his shoulders to release the pressure. Atlas, to his sorrow did so. Hercules left.

12. The Descent to the Underworld: Cerberus, the three headed dog that guarded the gates to Hades was Hercules' next quarry. He was to subdue the animal with only his hands. When he did this and brought the snarling beast to Erystheus, the king ordered him to take the dog back.

Heracles adventures were far from over once he had completed his twelve propitiating labors. He traveled widely, remarried, and continued to fight beast and foe. But Hera beat him in the end . . . or did she? Finally, Hercules ordered a large pyre built and he let himself be consumed by the flames. He was then welcomed to the land of the gods by his father, the mighty Zeus.

Picture Books: Hercules

Gates, Doris. (1975). *Mightiest of Morals: Heracles.* Illustrated by Richard Cuffari. New York: The Viking Press. This plainly written text would appeal to middle and upper-middle elementary school age children. The illustrations are also plain, black and white drawings that leave sufficient to the imagination to make their examination interesting. Much information is provided.

Lasky, Catherine. (1997). *Hercules.* Illustrated by Mark Hess. New York: Hyperion Books for Children. Lasky has compressed, with considerable success given the constricting nature of such an approach, the broad and sweeping tale of Hercules' life and adventures into an illustrated text. She has managed to convey a sense of Hera's continuing venom, the physical strength of the man who became a god, and the awesome labors Hercules underwent. A full accounting of each of the twelve tasks set by King Eurystheus has not been presented, which does tend to make the reader feel a little "shorted."

Riordan, James. (1997). *The Twelve Labors of Hercules*. Illustrated by Christina Balit. Brookfield, CT: The Millbrook Press. The Greeks called the son of Zeus, Herakles, meaning "Glory to Hera." This was rather a strange epithet considering that Hera was not his mother. In easy fashion Riordan has documented Hera's jealousy and the way it subsequently led to the hero having to undertake twelve extraordinary labors.

Myths and Legends From the North

From the north came the myths and legends of a people sometimes called the Norse and also known as the Vikings. The latter term means "fighting men" or "settling men" and indeed a great deal of both fighting and settling was undertaken during the Viking Age, generally regarded as lasting between 780–1070. During this time the people of the north attacked villages in Britain, France, Germany, and Spain and frequently settled in those countries.

The stories of the gods of the Vikings are celebrated in two books written in Iceland and known collectively as the Eddas. The older was written in poetry in 1056 and the more modern text in prose in 1640. The stories they contain, particularly those associated with the creation of the world, appear quite strange to modern man.

Norsemen believed the world was formed in a bottomless deep out of mist and the waters of twelve rivers that flowed to the center of the world. Freezing layer upon layer, the water became ice and the great deep was thus filled. The light and warmth of the south flowed over the ice and vapors arose and formed clouds. Out of these clouds emerged Ymir, the frost giant, and a cow, Audmula, whose milk sustained the wretched being and his children. For her part, the cow was nourished when she licked the salt from the ice.

It was during the act of licking the ice that Audmula uncovered a god, a beautiful, fully formed being. With his wife, the daughter of one of the giant race, this god found in the primordial wilderness produced three sons—Odin, Vili, and Ve. In time they were to kill Ymir and dispatch his being so it became the earth as we know it. His body was made into the earth, his blood the ocean, his bones the mountains, and his skull the heavens. Ymir's eyebrows formed the area known as Midgard or mid earth which in time became man's home.

Norsemen also once believed that long ago the gods that ruled over man lived in a place called Asgard (AHZ-gahrd). It was a place of great beauty with farms and orchards, hills, and valleys. Asgard was accessible only by Bifröst, (BEE-frost) a rainbow bridge. The gods could gallop on their mounts over this bridge with one exception—Thor, god of war. He rode an iron chariot pulled by enormous goats which would have tested Bifröst beyond endurance. The god Heimdall constantly guarded the bridge and no enemy could breach it. Heimdall's hearing was so acute that he could hear the wool growing on a sheep's back; his sight so keen he could see in the dark. It was Heimdall's sorry duty to blow a trumpet at the end of the world.

Odin, the wise father of the gods and men, and called All-Father, had built the beautiful city of Asgard which consisted of gold and silver palaces, from which he could look out over the whole world. And the world of the Norse is a complicated one; it includes men, giants, and dwarfs as well as many mysterious creatures.

The gloomy land that was the home of the giants was called Jotunheim (YOH-tun-hame) and was said to lie among the roots of Yggdrasil (EGG-drah-sil), the giant ash tree which united the heavens, the earth, and the underworld. The goal of the Frost-Giants and Hill-Giants was always to destroy the gods and mankind. In the caves beneath the mountains lived a race of dwarfs who were renowned as skilled craftsmen, particularly jewelers, but not known for their friendliness to either gods or man.

Man lived in a kingdom known as Midgard situated below Asgard and on the ragged edges of the world where earth and sky meet. Man was created by Odin and his two brothers, Ve and Vili, to live in Midgard when they discovered themselves dissatisfied with that land. They felt their creation incomplete and so fashioned people to give it life and impulse. The man and the woman first made out of ash and elm trees respectively were given the breath of life, sharp wits, and feeling. All people, states Norse myth, come from these early beings. Encircling Midgard is a giant serpent by the name of Jormungard. He swallows the earth at the day of doom.

Odin spent much time in Valhalla, (Val-HAHL-lah) an immense banqueting hall with walls of spears and a roof of shields. With him was the army of heroes, men who had died bravely in battle. Those slain had been selected and brought to heaven by beautiful maidens called Valkyries (VAHL-kure-reez) atop their airy horses. Such was the size of the hall that it had 500 doors, each of them wide enough to allow 800 people to march in abreast. All brave men under arms were to be needed on the day of doom to fight off the giants and so Valhalla was beyond immense. One of the typical meals served was a boar which magically came to life again once it had been eaten!

Odin sat on a high seat at the head of the feasts, eating nothing, with his two ravens on his shoulders. Known as Hugin and Munin, or *Thought and Memory*, the birds would fly out daily into the world and report at night on what they had seen. Odin remained abreast of what was happening in this fashion, but often the All-Father would himself visit the world. He was known to rage through the forests in autumn on his eight-legged horse, Slepnir (SLEP-neer) who was the fastest horse in the universe.

Odin was a strange, solemn, aloof figure. He was always pondering how to put off the day of doom known as Ragnorak (RAHG-nah-rock) when all heaven and earth, including himself, would be destroyed. In his search for wisdom to stave off this horror, the All-Father went to the Well of Wisdom and begged its guardian, Mimir (MEE-meer) for a draught. Mimir, whose head was severed from his body but who was nonetheless wise, told him he would have to pay for it with one of his eyes. Odin did.

Odin passed on much of the hard won knowledge he gained to men and was always the benefactor of humankind. For instance, he passed on the recipe for the mead drunk by the skalds or storytellers stolen from the giants; anyone who tasted it would sound like a poet.

Odin had a famous son, a legendary warrior named Thor, who waged a constant war against the giants. His most prized possession was a hammer named Mjolnir that would always return to him. This hammer is sometimes regarded as being symbolic of law and order. In addition, Thor owned a rare belt that doubled the strength of the wearer whenever it was donned.

Frey is the most celebrated god in the Norse pantheon, as he presides over sun and rain and the bounty that these elements provide from the earth. Freya, his sister is also celebrated as a patron of life and love. She adores music, flowers, fairies, and lovers! But it is to Bragi that the title of poet goes. He enjoys the society of the goddess Idun (or Iduna), who is entrusted with the magic, restorative apples the gods may eat when they feel themselves growing old and weary.

Of all the gods that lived in Asgard, Loki, the foster brother of Odin who came from the giants, alone wished malice on the community causing its downfall and the dreadful day of Ragnorak. Aiding in this destruction were two of three grotesque children Loki had sired—the Midgard Serpent, Jormungand, who ate the earth, and Fenrir, a wolf who had been fettered and rose up to kill Odin and swallow the sun. The third child fathered by Loki is Hela or Death!

Figure 2. The Norse Pantheon

Major Gods, Giants, and Dwarfs	*Characteristic*
Odin, the All-Father	The greatest of all gods who presided over the Hall of the Slain, Valhalla. Worked to stave off the day of doom.
Frigg	Odin's wife who knew the future but did not reveal it.
Balder	Most loved of all gods concerned with gentleness and beauty.
Bragi	God of poetry and husband of Idun, the keeper of the golden apples of youth.
Freya	Goddess of fertility. She drove a chariot pulled by cats and owned a magic falcon suit.
Heimdall	Keeper of the gods who announced the end of the world by blowing on his trumpet.

cont.

Hymir	Hymir was a giant and owner of an enormous cauldron desired by Thor.
Idun	A goddess who was keeper of the golden apples of youth.
Loki	A trickster giant who lived with the gods. He caused the world of the gods to end. His children were grotesque.
Thor	God of thunder who was the strongest of all gods. Thor had a mighty hammer that would always return to him.
Thrym	Thrym was a giant who once stole Thor's hammer. Loki helps Thor get it back by tricking the giant.
Tyr	God who sacrificed his hand to the wolf, Fenrir.
Ymir	The first frost giant formed from ice and fire. It was from Ymir's body that the universe was made.

Picture Books and Illustrated Texts: Norse Myths

Climo, Shirley. (1994). *Stolen Thunder*. Illustrated by Alexander Koshkin. New York: Clarion Books. "Long ago in the morning of time, there lived a people called the Norse." So begins a dramatic and funny story. When Thor, the Thunder-maker, loses his fearful magic hammer named Mjolnir, to Thrym, the king of giants, he sets about to retrieve it with the able help of Loki. Both gods practice a deceit to do it. Koshkin's illustrations do the tale justice.

Lock, Kath and Frances Kelly. (1995). *Freya*. Illustrated by Carol McLean-Carr. Mission Hills, CA: Australian Press. The goddess of love, Freya, loved above all things her husband, Odur, and the handsome god loved her in return. Freya also loved beautiful jewelry and it was a shining piece that compromised her marriage. When Odur was away the three Dwarfs of Darkness trapped Freya with a glorious necklace. Their price was a kiss each. Loki, the mischief maker, observed these events, reported them to Odur who left his unhappy wife much grieved. She searches for him to this day, her tears falling as drops of gold. "That is why, even today, gold is found in many parts of the world as a reminder of Freya's undying love."

Osborne, Mary Pope. (1996). *Favorite Norse Myths*. Illustrated by Troy Howell. New York: Scholastics Inc. Osborne, a fine reteller of myth and legend, has brought to younger readers 14 of the classic Norse myths. She begins with the story of the creation of the nine worlds and ends with the "Twilight of the Gods." Some of the stories are lesser known; how the giantess Skadi chose her husband, for example. Others such as Odin's quest for wisdom are more familiar to the casual reader. The author has provided the reader with full background on the origin of the tales and the life and history of the Vikings who gave them birth. Howell's illustrations, based on primitive representations of Viking art, are striking.

Philip, Neil. (1996). *Odin's Family*. Illustrated by Maryclare Foa. New York: Orchard Books. Neil has provided the reader with a comprehensive and accessible group of stories. He begins with the creation story and makes account of the many adventures of the deities to the end of the Aesir in the battle of Ragnorak. An afterward, which gives information about the gods of the north who were merely a reflection of the war-like people who created them, is most useful.

Arthurian Tales

Arthur, the great spirited and mythical king is claimed by both England and Wales and is regarded as a Celt. While there is no doubt about the existence of warrior kings, there is no proof that a person such as Arthur of the legend existed. In any event, this king above all others has now been firmly associated with the age of knights and chivalry.

Most stories about King Arthur and his court were developed over the middle ages, that period of time generally calculated to be the 5th century after the fall of the Roman Empire to the 15th century. One of the first to give these tales of the warrior king in Europe in the early Medieval period some coherence in a major work was Geoffrey of Monmouth. His text called, *Historia regum Britanniae* (c.1135), was a somewhat suspect history based on Celtic tradition that has at the centerpiece the glorious exploits of King Arthur. For example, Arthur is believed to have engaged the invading Saxons during the 5th and 6th centuries at least twelve times and slain many men with his own hands.

Various writers added to the cycle after Geoffrey's contribution and the legend was further developed. For example, Chrétien de Troyes in his poetry (c. 1160-1180) develops Arthur as a romantic and introduced the theme of the Holy Grail, the dish of the last supper given by Christ to Joseph of Arimathea. The next author of prominence known to have contributed to the Arthurian legend and believed to have crystallized it is Sir Thomas Malory, born into the age of knight errantry. His work entitled *Morte d'Arthur* was published in "the lX yere of the reyegne of King Edward the furth," (1459-1470). It was Malory who kindled the ongoing love affair the public has had with Arthur's kingdom, and the stories he put to print have continued to enchant people ever since. Given the wealth of stories, that are now available particularly in accessible picture book format, the romance will not likely fade again any time soon.

Some background of the customs of the period provides flesh to the stories of King Arthur. The word "chivalry" derives from the French *"cheval,"* a horse.

Knight originally referred to a boy or servant but came to mean a title a man earned after a long period of training in martial arts. He was generally permitted to take up arms at about the age of 21. Once admitted, a knight became a mounted warrior in the service of a noble of rank and means. In times of war, of course, the knight fought in the cause of his champion but in times of peace he wandered the country side. These wandering soldiers were called knights-errant and were generally welcomed fully into the chilly and sober castles of the nobility since they provided much sought after entertainment.

The King Arthur Story

The tales about King Arthur actually begin before his birth with the wizard, Merlin of Wales. Merlin was a strange boy born of a spirit father and a princess. He had "the sight" which he used to save himself from the bile of an invader and usurper, Vortigern. Merlin was able to explain to Vortigern why the battle tower he was trying to build was flawed; it was being constructed above two sleeping dragons, one red, the other white. When they were released from their stone eggs, they fought till the red dragon died and the white flew off to be free.

It was not long before the prophecy of the fighting dragons was fulfilled. Vortigern was burned in the tower that was meant to protect him after being attacked by an army under the banner of a white dragon. A leader who was to be the father of the greatest king of all then rose to power. This man was Uther who took on the moniker Pendragon, or head of the dragon.

Arthur was born to Uther Pendragon and a beautiful woman seduced by the ruler by the name of Igrayne. The baby was taken at an early age into foster care (a common Celtic custom). At Merlin's request a rural squire, Sir Hector and his wife cared for the child, along with their own son, Kay, until Arthur was sixteen and forced by circumstances to take up the crown.

The process by which Arthur was selected to become king was as magical and eerie as Merlin himself. At the time of Arthur's ascendancy to the throne, the land was ruled by the widowed Igrayne. But it was a troubled kingdom and one in need of a strong leader. Igrayne decreed under Merlin's guidance that a new king would be chosen in London at Christmas. In the midst of the crowds at Westminster Abbey stood a slab of marble bearing a sword with a mysterious inscription. Only the true and rightful heir to the throne would be able to remove the sword from its stone scabbard. As Merlin knew, it was to be the beardless boy known as Arthur who did so.

The young and fearful boy king proved to be a lion in battle and it was his fighting spirit along with the help provided him by Merlin that won him the allegiance of the many sceptics in his kingdom. Arthur was protected by a wide, wondrous, unbreakable sword known as Excalibur. Of more value to the royal though was the jeweled scabbard. While he was wearing it he could not be injured.

Arthur's long rule was marked by both glory and dishonor. His glory was the establishment of the order of knights who were bound by oath to be chivalrous and to work for the common good. It was these men who fought dragons, giants, and evil in general to make the land peaceful and prosperous. Although most knights were noble, the honor of being the greatest belonged to Lancelot who was much loved by both Arthur and his wife, Guinevere.

Lancelot returned Guinevere's love despite his best efforts to contain his affection. This relationship was partly instrumental in bringing the era of the Knights of the Round Table to a close and into the realm of the mythical. Its destruction was aided and abetted by an evil sorceress by the name of Morgan, the youngest of Igrayne's three daughters, and a usurper called Mordred.

But there are more glories to be spoken of before the Arthur tales are over. The seeking of the Holy Grail by Sir Galahad, Lancelot's son, and the death of the king and Mordred complete the cycle. In addition each of the knights has his own story or stories, so the King Arthur tales are indeed rich.

Some of these stories are available in picture book and illustrated text format and suitable for children. They tend to be long and are suitable for older readers.

Main Characters in the Arthurian Legends

Arthur. As noted previously, the warrior king of the Medieval cycle is essentially the creation of Geoffrey of Monmouth. Central to his reign was the establishment of a fellowship of knights who sat around a Round Table. None was elevated over the other around such a piece of furniture.

An interesting aside is worth noting here. A famous round table top is on display on the east wall of Winchester Castle, England. It is a great cross section of a huge oak with spokes extending from the center to the rim. At the end of each line are names of the valiant knights who joined their king. Radiocarbon analysis dates the table to the fourteenth century, but the central design on it dates from the sixteenth century and consists of a double rose, red and white, above which is painted a crowned head. While it was no doubt intended to be King Arthur, it resembles closely a youthful Henry VIII.

Arthur is one of those select heroes who was believed by many of the populace of the Middle Ages not to have died. Rather, he is merely at rest and will rouse when the country is again facing a national peril and has need of him. He is typically reputed to be asleep, along with his knights in a cave somewhere. All will stir when there is a crises needing his courage and cunning.

Merlin. Merlin is the wizard, a strange character who was born in the wilds of Wales to a woman and a spirit, sometimes called an eldritch, whose task is to watch over the fledgling kingdom of King Arthur. Arthur sorely misses his friend when Merlin deems it time to live with Lady Nemue, the lady of his life who is also known as "The Lady of the Lake."

Merlin is associated with many magical acts and places, the most significant of which are the famous pillars of Stonehenge in England. These ancient and magic stones known as the "Magic Ring" were originally located in Ireland and sacred to the people. Merlin sailed to the Emerald Isle with two hundred men and instructed them how to move the weight with levers and cranes. No one disturbed the labor for Merlin had used his powers and made time stand still. When the ships reached Salisbury Plain, the stones were levered to a moving road of logs and Stonehenge was formed.

Women of the Arthurian Cycles

Guinevere. is Arthur's wife and the beautiful daughter of King Leodegrance. She is linked in the modern mind with infidelity as she left her husband in favor of his knight, Lancelot. She began her marriage very much in love with Arthur but her inability to bear an heir placed the two, unwillingly, at a distance. Lancelot, her gallant champion, rescued her from the horrible fate of burning at the stake when their illicit relationship was finally revealed by the knight Gawain. Guinevere ended her days as a nun and was buried at the edge of the lake by her faithful lover at the spot where Arthur was last seen alive.

Queen Morgana le Fay. is Arthur's half-sister; they share the same mother, Igrayne. She is a sorceress of some malevolence who plots the king's downfall in revenge for the death of her father, the Duke of Cornwall. She believes the duke's passing to have been caused by Merlin. She also wishes to have the throne.

Elayne. or Elaine is a maiden who desperately loves Sir Lancelot and bears him a most famous child, Sir Galahad, the most chivalrous of all the knights. Sir Lancelot cannot return her affection and the fair lady passes away with grief.

The Lady of the Lake. is the Lady Nemue. She is the lady of the mysterious lake which surrounds the island of Avalon and separates life from death. Lady Nemue, appears under many different names and features in some tellings as the king's guardian when Arthur is in danger. She is sometimes regarded as Merlin's love.

Knights of the Round Table

The knights of the Round Table earned their place. One way to earn such a seat was to prove a worthy opponent in jousting tournaments. The knights, whose names appeared miraculously on the Round Table at Merlin's command, are too numerous to name and only the significant characters have been listed here.

Lancelot. is the knight above all others, an opponent without equal. He mysteriously appeared at a tournament and became Queen Guinevere's champion wearing her colors in competition. His adventures were numerous and gloriously celebrated, but he won notice when he became the Queen's illicit lover. He was also the father of the knight who was to secure the Holy Grail, Sir Galahad. Lancelot's life was not an easy one; he spent many years in exile trying to escape his feelings for Guinevere, was forced into rescuing her from the stake when their relationship was made public, and eventually ended his life as a monk. He buried Guinevere.

Gawain. is the son of Lord Loth of Orkney and a nephew to Arthur on his mother's side. He is an early character in the Arthurian stories and was regarded in these tales as a chivalrous hero who is both youthful and graceful. But in Malory's iteration of the legends, which tended to fix the tradition into literary form, he tends to be less favorably portrayed. It is partly the actions of Gawain that bring down the wonderful kingdom of Camelot and the death of the famous king.

In the various iterations of the *Gawain and the Green Knight* tales portrayed below, Sir Gawain is unable to separate the Green Knight's head from the body, the neck is impervious to the sword. In the original story the head and body part company amiably. In Celtic lore a severed head was believed to have magic power in as much as it could make prophecies, curse, protect, and most significantly, reunite with the trunk of the person from which it came.

Galahad. Sir Galahad is the illegitimate son of Lancelot and the Lady Elayne and supposedly the last descendent of Joseph of Arimathea. He is regarded as the most chivalrous and most virtuous knight in the fellowship in Medieval Britain, and his place at the Round Table was a highly honored one. It was called the *Siege Perilous* and was reserved for the knight who was so pure he would someday find the Holy Grail, the cup or dish used by Jesus Christ at the Last Supper.

Mordred. Mordred is usually depicted as nephew to King Arthur and sometimes as son. He is of an evil disposition and has been planted in the court by the sorceress Morgana Le Fay. He seizes power when Arthur leaves for France and builds up a following. He is killed by Arthur in the battle that ensues when the rightful king returns home. Tragically before Mordred dies, he kills his former liege lord.

Picture Books: Arthurian Legends

Below are summaries of some of the Arthurian stories that have been written in picture book format. In the fashion of legends, the same tales sometimes differ one from another in their particulars.

Curry, Jane Louise. (1993). *The Christmas Knight*. Illustrated by DiAnne DiSalvo-Ryan. New York: Margaret K. McElderry Books. This book predates Arthur's reign and is set "in the time when his father, Uther, was king." A merry knight, Sir Cleges sponsors a fine feast each Christmas until he is impoverished. Then he is shunned. When King Uther visits his nearby castle to celebrate the festive season, they are not invited to the party. Quick wit and a miracle, a gift from God of red summer cherries on a snowy Christmas morning, gained Cleges access to the king and a recognition of which he was deserving. Sir Cleges is dubbed the Christmas Knight, lord of Cardiff Castle, and host of a feast of the homeless and hungry, in the king's own name.

Hastings, Selina. (1985). *Sir Gawain and the Loathly Lady*. Illustrated by Juan Wijngaard. New York: Lothrop, Lee & Shepard Books. King Arthur is held to a wager by the evil Black Knight. He will die if he cannot tell the knight what it is in the world a lady wants. A repulsive old hag tells the king what he needs to know (a lady wants her own way), but her price for the information is high. She wants a chivalrous knight for her husband. Gallant and handsome Gawain offers to become the groom. The pity felt by all for the young man turns to joy when it is discovered that the bride is actually a beautiful maiden under enchantment. By marrying her, and giving her her own way, Gawain has freed them to live in great happiness. (The loathly lady is the feminine equivalent of the ugly beast who is a handsome man under an evil spell.)

Hieatt, Constance. (1967). *Sir Gawain and the Green Knight*. Illustrated by Walter Lorraine. New York: Thomas Y. Crowell Company. Sir Gawain makes a noble offer one evening at a feast hosted by King Arthur. He alone takes up the strange challenge made by the Green Knight who bursts upon their company. Sir Gawain will chop off the head of the Green Knight in one blow and allow the Green Knight to do likewise to him a year later. The air is perfectly still when the gallant knight takes his blow. It is clean. But the challenger picks up his rolling head and rides off. One year later, Sir Gawain must fulfill his promise and he sets off with a heavy heart. He is in for more than he expects. A coy seduction scene may make this book unsuitable for younger children.

Heyer, Carol. (1991). *Excalibur*. Illustrated by the author. Nashville, Tennessee: Ideals Children's Books. Heyer provides an account of how the sword typically thought of as *Excalibur* was given to the king by the Lady Nemue, Lady of the Lake. It is story that explores the mystique of Arthur. In this iteration Arthur initially thought the sword, given to him at Merlin's request by the Lady of the Lake, would make him invincible but he slowly began to realize that it was only his inner strength that could do that.

Hodges, Margaret. (1990). *The Kitchen Knight*. Illustrated by Trina Schart Hyman. New York: Holiday House. This is a retelling of the first part of the cycle around Sir Gareth of Orkney. Gareth, a nephew of the King, poses as a kitchen hand to discover his true friends. During the period of self-imposed servility, he prepares to become a true knight. When the opportunity is right he proves himself well and truly worthy by virtue of his courteous and gallant behavior toward women and his bravery in facing his foes. Besides winning himself a place at King Arthur's side, Gareth secures the heart and hand of the fair maiden, Linesse.

Sabuda, Robert. (1995). *Arthur and the Sword*. Illustrated by the author. New York: Atheneum Books for Young Readers. Sabuda's retelling of this famous story is distinguished by luminous "stained glass" illustrations that make the reader feel as though he or she is indeed looking through interesting windows. An author's note states that the sword Arthur pulled from the rock is called *Excalibur* which is thought to mean "to free from the stone." It had to be drawn many times by the beardless boy before people could believe that he would be worthy of being king. This account is at variance with the commonly told one that Excalibur is the sword that was given to him by the Lady of the Lake.

San Souci, Robert, D., (1996). *Young Lancelot*. Illustrated by Jamichael Henterly. New York: Doubleday. San Souci has detailed the life of Lancelot from the time he was orphaned as a young baby until he proves himself worthy of becoming a knight at Arthur's table. He was to become the greatest knight of them all, but before he could do so he had to overcome his arrogance and pride. His foster mother, Niniane, The Lady of the Lake, sets him a test during which he could prove both his courage and his compassion. Having passed the test Lancelot can not only take his place as a knight but he can also learn his true identity as a king's son.

San Souci, Robert, D., (1993). *Young Guinevere*. Illustrated by Jamichael Henterly. New York: Doubleday. The influences of the childhood upon the gracious woman who was to become Arthur's wife is the focus of this story. While based on a variety of classic and contemporary sources the author admits to reflecting the "might-have-beens." This telling which invokes shapeshifting creatures and monsters conjures up a courageous girl who defends her father's castle against enemies as well as any trained soldier. She also becomes Arthur's bride against the wishes of the druid, Merlin. While full knowing the prophecy that she will bring down Arthur's Camelot, Guinevere cannot deny her destiny.

San Souci, Robert, D., (1990). *Young Merlin*. Illustrated by Daniel Horne. New York: Doubleday. San Souci's version of the childhood of the magician Merlin differs from Service's reviewed below but is no less compelling. Wonderfully luminous illustrations accompany the lengthy text.

Service, Pamela, F. (1990). *Wizard of Wind and Rock*. Illustrated by Laura Marshall. New York: Atheneum. This tale, set in the "wild winds and rocks of Wales," is the story of the boyhood of the wizard Merlin who was to assist King Arthur in his quest toward greatness and legend. Marshall's illustrations are as wild and romantic as the story.

Shannon, Mark. (1994). *Gawain and the Green Giant*. Illustrated by David Shannon. New York: G. P. Putnam's Sons. Shannon's interpretation of the old and oft-told story of how a gallant knight takes up the peculiar challenge at the Christmas celebration of the knights of the round table is appropriate for younger ages. The seduction scene that is part of the original story and Hieatt's interpretation noted above is adroitly avoided in this telling.

Talbot, Hudson, *King Arthur and the Round Table*. Illustrated by the author. New York: Morrow Junior Books. Perhaps the most accessible account of how Arthur took up his kingdom is told in the picture book written by Hudson Talbot and simply called, *King Arthur and the Round Table*. The lengthy text has a reverent majesty.

Watson, Richard Jesse. (1989). *Tom Thumb*. Illustrated by the author. San Diego: Harcourt Brace Jovanovich, Publishers. Watson introduces the diminutive folklore character of *Tom Thumb* into the Arthurian cycles via Merlin. The wizard came to a humble cottage disguised as a beggar. Noting the sadness of the couple, he inquired as to the reason. "I long for a child," the tearful wife declared, "even if the babe were no bigger than my husband's thumb." Amused by the idea Merlin granted the wish. The tiny little boy that was born never grew any bigger than thumb size but his adventures were gigantic. When the stout little warrior prevented a war between the king and the giant, Grumbong, he was knighted by Arthur himself and took his place at the Round Table.

Yolen, Jane. (1995). *Merlin and the Dragons*. Illustrated by Li Ming. New York: Cobblehill Books. Yolen's wondrous ability to tell a story is matched by Ming's facility with oils. Her illustrations of the legend of how the young Merlin, a strange, lonely, fatherless prince came of age in Wales are dramatic and breathtaking. *Merlin and the Dragons* is set as a story within a story. In addition to featuring the rise of the wizard, the tale portrays Arthur as a very young king. The comfort the young boy derives from finding out that he is indeed the rightful heir is reflected in the joyous, warm colors at the end of the tale.

Texts Cited

Anderson, D. A. (1991). *The Origins of Life on Earth*. Illustrated by Kathleen Atkins Wilson. Mt. Airy, MD: Sights Productions

Dee, R. (1991). *Tower to Heaven*. Illustrated by Jennifer Bent. New York: Henry Holt and Company.

Gerstein, M. (1986). *Tales of Pan*. New York: Harper & Row.

Guard, D. (1977). *Deidre*. Illustrated by Gretchen Guard. Milbrae, California: Celestial Arts.

McCaughrean, G. (1996). *The Golden Hoard*. New York: Simon & Schuster.

Yeats, W. B. (1888). *Irish Fairy and Folk Tales*. New York: Random House.

3

Mythical Creatures and Fantastic Beasts

The Middle Ages was the time when belief in the fantastic beast was supreme. People of this period lived in a world circumscribed by the immediacy of their environment and the word of writers. Pliny the Elder, a Roman naturalist, was referred to for many generations as an authority on the natural world despite the fact that he had never seen many of the creatures he described. In addition, the storytellers of yore elaborated upon the creatures that never were in tales handed down generation to generation. Such a practice created atmosphere and an erroneous fauna!

Some of these mysterious creatures and fantastic beasts have been given life all across the globe; the dragon, the mermaid, the fairy, and the unicorn are very much alive in both eastern and western cultures. Other creatures, such as the Phoenix, the wondrous male bird that dies every five hundred years and is reborn from its own ashes, are well known but not widely embraced. Yet other creations are local to a given culture or area; Tengu are intensely Japanese, for instance. They are strange woodland creatures who are both helpful and mischievous.

Mention is made below of some of these beings, as is reference to folk tales about them, where available, that children will enjoy.

Unicorns

The unicorn, one of the most charming of all mythical beasts, is variously described as horse-like or having the appearance of a goat with a distinguishing horn on its forehead. It is perhaps the most lingering of all the creatures of the human imagination and was not completely consigned to the mythical and fantastic until the early nineteenth century. In 1827 a French naturalist, Baron Georges Cuvier, laid down as a rule of nature that it was impossible for an animal with a cleft hoof to have a horn growing in the middle of its forehead. He based his claim on numerous anatomical studies with goats and sheep.

Lore about the solitary unicorn is part of every culture, but the beliefs tend to differ slightly in the east and in the west.

Eastern Unicorn: The Chinese call the unicorn ki'-lin or simply lin and claim it is king among beasts. They believe it comes to man from heaven and visits only at intervals as an omen of good or as a signal for the end of an illustrious period. The first reported sighting of the horned beast in the Middle Kingdom was during in the reign of Fu Hsi about 2800 B.C. A unicorn approached the emperor as he sat at the banks of the Yellow River. On the creature's back were signs which Fu Hsi copied and subsequently used as the first written language of China. Fu Hsi's reign was marked by other singular accomplishments such as the invention of musical instruments and the development of animal husbandry. The next emperor, Shên Nung, never did see the unicorn but his successor, Huang Ti, did and in keeping with the belief that the unicorn signaled a great era he achieved a good deal. He regulated the calendar, was the first builder of houses and towns, and expanded the empire through commerce. Huang Ti reportedly rode to eternity on the back of the gracious unicorn and then the country slipped into turmoil.

Two thousand years later a unicorn appeared to the mother of the sage Confucius before his birth in the sixth century B.C. In his mouth the beast was carrying a great tablet of jade with the inscription that the expected baby would be a throneless king. The unicorn also appeared to the philosopher just before his death. Again the country slipped into decline.

The unicorn's presence was felt in China many centuries later. In 1415 the emperor Yung Loh came to the throne. He was an adventurer and sent his ships to places they had not been before. One of the vessels bearing his colors went to Africa and the crew returned with a giraffe thinking it was the hallowed ki'-lin. The emperor, knowing the difference, accepted it as a unicorn anyway given the long necked beast was such a curiosity.

The Japanese unicorn is known as the sin-you and has a similar gentle nature to the ki'-lin but a different appearance; it is more lion-like, being thick-maned and tawny. It also has a singular ability—to tell right from wrong. There is a story that an old sage by name of Kau You would call on the sin-you when he had to decide capital cases and could not trust his own judgement. The unicorn would stand completely still and then fix his eyes on the accused. If guilty, he then would pierce him through the heart with a horn.

Western Unicorn: The Greek Ctesias was one of the first to describe the wondrous unicorn to the west. He accepted a post as physician in 416 B.C. in the court of Darius II, the King of Persia, from which he was to return seventeen years later to chronicle many events in two books. In a book about India, a country he had not visited, he was to state:

There are in India certain wild asses which are as large as horses, and larger. Their bodies are white, their heads are dark red, and their eyes dark blue. They have a horn on their forehead which is about a foot and a half in length. The dust filed from this horn is administered in a potion as a protection against deadly drugs.

This was information that was to be used and quoted in the following centuries by such notable Romans as Julius Caesar and the earlier mentioned Pliny the Elder.

About the second century B.C., 70 Hebrew scholars inadvertently perpetuated the unicorn myth when they translated the Old Testament into Greek for the first time. In the course of the work they came upon the Hebrew word R'em, a reference to a wild creature of considerable size and strength, which became translated into the one-horned. In later versions this reference became the unicorn. There are, for instance, seven clear references to the unicorn in the King James Bible. From Psalms xxii.21: "Save me from the lion's mouth; for thou has heard me from the horns of unicorns." (The beast in question was likely an extinct wild ox known as the urus or aurochs.)

During the Middle Ages, that period loosely defined as existing from the fifth to the fifteenth century, the stature of the unicorn grew to its height. Described in the Bestiary written by naturalist Physiologus, the beast was presented as a small but fierce animal that could be tamed only by the lure of a virgin.

Chief among the unicorn's virtues was the treasure of his brow; in the west the horn was believed able to discern poison. Frequently a piece of unicorn's horn or alicorn was placed on the table and any dishes that reacted by sweating or changing color were removed. The food was believed to be tainted and dangerous to eat. The supposed horn was often ground and the powder added to a liquid as an antidote to poison. Physicians in Europe in the sixteenth and seventeenth century also considered the alicorn a cure for the plague and other disorders such as epilepsy. Finally, the alicorn could make sweet the water fouled by any beast, particularly the serpent. All the unicorn had to do was to dip his horn into the water hole where animals drank and the liquid would become pure again.

The actual horn or the horn powder reputed to come from the unicorn is believed to have been the protruding spiraled tooth that grows from the head of a narwhal. It is often long and can project for a distance of ten feet.

The unicorn became symbolic over time. Its purity of nature and gentle habits, in combination with its strength and an ability to undo the malevolent acts of the evil serpent made it a common medieval symbol for Christ. The unicorn also symbolizes compassion. Adam was believed to have named the unicorn first when God bade him to give a name to all beasts on the earth he had created. God reached over and touched the pointed horn and from that moment the unicorn was elevated above all beasts. Adam and Eve would ride the unicorn's back in the Garden of Eden in their innocent state. When the transgressing couple were banished from their paradise God gave the unicorn the choice of staying where he was or going on to earth. The unicorn chose to go into the world and accept his share of hardships and for that act he is considered compassionate.

The unicorn is also a common figure in western heraldry. It has been consistently displayed on the Royal Arms of Scotland as a symbol of peace and, as of 1707 when the union between Scotland and England took place, stands in opposition to the fierce British lion. Two unicorns feature in the coat of arms of the Apothecaries Society which was formed in 1617. The symbolism for healing would have been well understood at the time.

Picture Books and Illustrated Texts: Unicorns

While there is much lore about the unicorn there appear to be few traditional or original folk tales.

Birrer, Cynthia & William Birrer. (1987). *The Lady and the Unicorn*. Illustrated by the authors. New York: Lothrop, Lee & Shepard Books. The well noted friendship between unicorns and young girls are featured in this tale based on the famous millefleurs tapestries. The illustrations they executed from textiles and stitchery are reminiscent of the intricate stitchery that is part of the collection. This story centers around a beautiful young girl, Teresa, who comes to live with her uncle, Prince Zizim, who is residing in exile. Of all the people in the castle only the beautiful and chaste Teresa could see the unicorn. She befriends him. But still the creature is lonely and one day begins to weep. When Teresa shows him in a mirror how truly beautiful he is, the enchantment under which the animal had been living is broken. In the place of the beast is a handsome prince!

Cooper, Gail. (1981). *One Unicorn*. Illustrated by the author. New York: E.P. Dutton. Gail Cooper has featured a princess by name of Alicia in her original folk tale. Alicia is the much loved daughter of the widowed king who was warned during a prophecy that he could never fully protect the girl, and the pain and sorrow she would endure would make her wise. It came to pass. Alicia found and befriended a unicorn. The pair were inseparable and would remain so as long as Alicia never lied to the magnificent beast. The princess did not until she fell in love. Wishing to spend all her time with Prince Nicholas she fibbed that she had forgotten their meetings. "Your time of innocence is over," said the unicorn, whereupon he exposed himself to the hunter's arrows. The ending is comforting nonetheless.

Coville, Bruce and Katherine. (1979). *Sarah's Unicorn*. Illustrated by the authors. New York: J.B. Lippincott. Sarah is a sad and lonely character whose life takes on a whole new meaning after she becomes friends with a unicorn in the forest. "Oakhorn" teaches the little girl to converse with animals and Sarah makes friends with a little ladybug, Mrs. Bunjy. Such happiness is threatened when Sarah's witch aunt, Mag, suspects the child of having access to magic and follows her into the night forest. Mag's delight at the sight of the unicorn is unbounded. Aware of the value of the horn she attempts to cut it off, an attempt that is thwarted at the last minute by Mrs. Bunjy. The result of this intervention is happier than could be imagined.

de Paola, Tomie. (1995). *The Unicorn and the Moon*. Illustrated by the author. Parsippany, New Jersey: Silver Press. "*The Unicorn and the Moon* is a tale about strange creatures long ago." Besides a rather vain unicorn, a griffin, a legendary half-eagle and half-lion fearful to look at, is featured. Together the creatures endeavor with a variety of strategies to free a trapped moon from between two hills, to no avail. It is the alchemist to whom the unicorn appeals who succeeds by fooling the hills with a trick and a sleight of hand! Silvery, blue illustrations feature in this tale set at night. The mystique of the evening is maintained with the silver end papers in the text.

Giblin, James Cross. (1991). *The Truth About Unicorns*. Illustrated by Michael McDermott. New York: HarperCollins Publisher. This is a reference written expressly for children. In friendly and accessible style that reads more like a story than nonfiction, the text presents the reader with significant history about the mythical and wondrous beast. There is a particularly interesting section about the famous Unicorn Tapestries and the significance and enduring impact of the work. Included in the text are woodcuts and illustrations from many sources.

Hathaway, Nancy. (1980). *The Unicorn*. New York: The Viking Press. Woven within the information and lore about the mythical beast are stories that would serve as suitable read alouds. For example, there is a fascinating retelling of a tale called *The Unicorn-Boy of India*, the story of the offspring of a holy man and a unicorn who saves a kingdom from a fearful king and drought. This is a useful reference text.

Mayer, Marianna. (1982). *The Unicorn and the Lake*. Illustrated by Michael Hague. New York: Dial Books for Young Readers. Mayer's version of the legend of the unicorn is based on three historical sources upon which she elaborates in a note preceding the tale. The lavishly illustrated story is set long ago when all animals, including the white unicorn live in harmony. But men drive the unicorn high into the mountains and his vanishing causes the magic to pass. Life becomes a desperate struggle to survive as the venomous serpent preys on those around him and a drought guts the land. When the animals' cries of distress reach the unicorn, he emerges from his mountain den and pierces the clouds with his horn to bring rain. All life forms are glad except the serpent who lives in the lake. The raging battle that ensues results in the unicorn gaining dominance over the serpent.

Dragons

Until four hundred years ago man hand little scientific knowledge but a lot of "evidence" for the existence of dragons. Large dinosaur bones were regarded as the remains of these mysterious creatures, and natural phenomena such as an erupting volcano was believed to indicate the presence of the beast nearby. As late as the sixteenth century, scientists were still listing several varieties of dragon as part of the known fauna.

Eastern and western dragons are viewed differently and have dissimilar characters. The dragon of the west is associated with much that is negative in life while their eastern cousins are benevolent.

Western Dragons: Western dragons are generally thought of as being large and lizard-like in appearance with scales and vertically attached wings that can open and close. The capacity to fly is not exercised all that often as most of these monsters prefer to sit in or near a cave guarding their vast supply of gold.

The notion that dragons are keepers of treasure is a very old one and goes back at least to the ancient Greeks. Ladon is one such dragon monster. He was believed to watch over the golden apples in the Garden of the Hesperides needed by Hercules as part of his labors. But to dream of dragons was a good sign according to Artemidorus, a Greek writer of the second century B.C. He claimed that dreaming of such beasts meant that wealth was imminent and prosperity assured!

Western dragons can also breathe fire, a capability that has been used to destroy whole cities. Furthermore, their fiery, sulphurous breath is deadly to all who come within contact. It is frequently turned on those hapless, brave souls who would attack the dragon who has appropriated the town water supply, a common trick when the flesh of humans was desired.

For the reasons noted above western dragons are the most feared of all fabulous beasts and have been so all through history. They epitomize evil, representing every reprehensible trait known to man. In short, the dragon is cruel and without any redeeming features, and its association with Satan is well justified. Perhaps the only value the dragon has for humans is its blood; some believed that a few drops of that substance will enable people to understand the language of birds and make them privy to some of the wisdom of beasts.

What the dragon has done for folk tales is to provide a foil for many Christian heroes and a means to sainthood. The most famous of all dragon slayers is Saint George, the patron saint of England; another is Saint Leonard of France. The latter brave and adventurous fighter preferred his own company after battle and won permission from his King, Clovis, to live a solitary life in the woods. The dragon who lived in the forest was enraged at the intrusion on his privacy and demanded the interloper leave. Saint Leonard failed to hear the dragon's demand so the beast destroyed his hut. A furious three-day fight ensued before good was to triumph over evil. When the battle was over the blood spilled by the saint became the lovely flower, lilly of the valley.

Not all encounters between dragons and saints have resulted in bloodshed, however. In years gone by some regarded the Loch Ness Monster as a dragon. Saint Columba was visiting the famous lake about 565 A.D. when the huge "beastie" appeared and headed toward one of his followers in the water. Columba intervened shouting at Nessie to resist. Indeed she did. She fled back to her underground lair and did not disturb the saint and his party again.

Dragons have frequently served as symbols of importance or portents of momentous events. It is said that Uther, father of the famed King Arthur, once had a vision of a flaming dragon in the skies directly above him. This was interpreted to mean that Uther would become king; he did so taking the name Pendragon or Dragon Head. His standard displayed a winged dragon. Merlin, the wizard who was to foster in the reign of Pendragon's son, King Arthur, was called as a very young boy by the evil interloper, Vortigen, to interpret the meaning of two dragons fighting on Salisbury Plain. One was red, the other white. Merlin explained that the rivers of Britain would run red with blood as Briton fought Saxon. Merlin's story of how this drama plays out is aptly explored in at least three fine picture books: one by Jane Yolen titled *Merlin and the Dragons,* another by Robert D. San Souci called *Young Merlin,* and another slightly different interpretation by Pamela Service called *Wizard of Wind and Rock.* (See chapter 2, *Western Myths.)*

Picture Books and Illustrated Texts: Western Dragons

Dugin, Andrej & Olga Dugina. (1993). *Dragon Feathers.* Illustrated by the authors. Charlottesville, Virginia: Thomasson-Grant. While the dragon may be a mean and disconcerting creature, his wife is sometimes depicted as a gentle soul. Such is the case in this whimsical Austrian tale. Henry, who goes to extraordinary lengths to win the hand of the beautiful daughter of the rich innkeeper, is charged to bring three golden feathers from the dragon who lives in the forest (and who normally eats people). Henry meets three people en route who each make a request. The gentle dragon's wife unexpectedly is Henry's accomplice. With her help he obtains the feathers, finds the answer to the three questions asked of him, and becomes a man of means now worthy of a wife. This story features glorious, gently bizarre illustrations that were two years in the making.

Fisher, Leonard Everett. (1990). *Jason and the Golden Fleece.* Illustrated by the author. New York: Holiday House. Sometimes a dragon-slayer is dependent upon the attentions of a goddess or sorceress to gain supremacy. Jason, of classical Greek folklore, is such a case. He was sent out to capture a golden fleece by his wicked cousin, Pelias, who had usurped Jason's right to the throne. Pelias, of course, could not believe that anyone could survive such a trial.

After many adventures the Argonauts arrived at the place where the fleece was guarded by a monstrous and sleepless dragon. Jason secured the help of the sorceress Medea, who lulled the monster into slumber with a magical lullaby. The hero was able to pluck the treasure from the tree on which it lay and beat a hasty retreat back to Greece to secure his throne.

Greene, Ellin. (1994). *Billy Beg and His Bull*. Illustrated by Kimberly Bucken Root. New York: Holiday House. Billy Beg (which means little), born the son of a king has more adventures in his lifetime than most people have in three. This story has all the trappings of a tall tale. Billy's pet bull dramatically saves him from his wicked stepmother and bequeaths him three magic gifts. They enable Billy to fend off three mighty giants, each one more ferocious than the last, and a fearsome dragon. This last act wins him the hand of the beautiful princess with whom he lives happily ever after. In a twist on the Cinderella story, it is Billy who plays coy and waits for the princess to come to him with his shoe that will identify him as the hero!

Haley, Gail E. (1988). *Jack and the Fire Dragon*. Illustrated by the author. New York: Crown Publishers, Inc. Poppyseed, the old storyteller, the teller of tales about Jack the tow-headed scamp who keeps turning young again, entertains her grandchildren with the tale of how her hero defeated Old Fire Dragaman, the dragon who lived under the mountain. In the process of vanquishing the formidable beast who wandered the forest and pillaged at will, Jack becomes wealthy and meets Jenny, a beautiful maiden who becomes his bride. Jack also forgives his two older jealous brothers for their malevolent treatment of him during his adventure, laughing at them because "he liked laughing better than he liked fighting."

Hodges, Margaret. (1984). *Saint George and the Dragon*. Illustrated by Trina Schart Hyman. Boston: Little, Brown and Company. This iteration of the story of the slaying of the hideous dragon by the patron saint of England is taken from Edmund Spenser's *Faerie Queen*. The text is somewhat lengthy and detailed for the picture book format, particularly the description of the three day battle between the foul monster and the knight. For this reason the book would be more suitable for older readers. Hyman's illustrations, which are detailed and dramatic, earned the prestigious Caldecott Medal.

McCaughrean, Geraldine. (1989). *Saint George and the Dragon*. Illustrated by Nicki Palin. New York: Doubleday. A calm Medieval English village turns into a horror after a dragon inhabits a nearby pool forcing the people into the city gates to avoid being eaten. Each day two sheep are loosed to satiate the monster in full knowledge that the supply is not boundless. Before the last sheep is gone the people begin to draw lots in a terrible lottery. Everyone has a chance of becoming the dragon's meal. Among the unlucky is Princess Sabra. Just as the scaly monster contemplates consuming her, a rider on a white horse across the hill distracts the beast and a furious battle ensues. The victorious stranger who refuses the hospitality of the village became known as St. George the dragon slayer, the patron saint of England.

Roth, Susan, L. (1996). *Brave Martha and the Dragon*. Illustrated by the author. New York: Dial Books for Young Readers. In France one of the Christian dragon-slayers of note is a woman. The redoubtable lady saved the folks of an ancient little village from a marauding monster. No one had been able to quell the beast, but Martha does by sheer will power and a long sash she wears over her simple shift. An author's note explains that this story is the basis for a festival held each year in Tarascon in Provence, an old town nestled by the banks of the River Rhône. It is known as the Fête de la Tarasque (the Fête of the Dragon) and is a joyous occasion in honor of the girl now known as Saint Martha.

Yolen, Jane. (1989). *Dove Isabeau*. Illustrated by Dennis Nolan. San Diego: Harcourt Brace Jovanovich. "On the cold northern shore of Craig's Cove, where the trees bear leaves only three months of the year, there stood a great stone castle with three towers. In the central tower lived a girl named Isabeau, and she was fair." The witch who married Dove Isabeau's father, jealous of the fair maiden, changed the girl into a cannibalistic dragon. In such a state Dove Isabeau was destined to circle her island home and all who came near the hideous beast were devoured, except one. He was the King's son, Kemp Owain who had always loved Dove. This love, along with a faithful white cat enabled the transformation of the dragon back to fair maiden and the destruction of the wicked witch. Yolen's story is a rather haunting one.

Eastern Dragons: Like unicorns dragons feature widely in the folk lore of the Orient but few stories about them appear to exist. In contrast to the monsters of the west they represent everything that is good and beautiful. Dragons of the Orient are numerous, much loved, and revered as symbols of wisdom and hidden knowledge that they will share willingly with their companions—emperors and sages.

An eastern dragon looks different from his western cousins. He is more reptilian in appearance but does not have wings. Nonetheless, he can fly, frequently leaping to heaven in one bound. Usually the eastern dragon has two horns which serve as ears and a head that resembles a horse. In addition, he can make himself invisible or change size. One of the mysteries associated with the appearance of the eastern dragon is the pearl-like globular object suspended in the air in front of or below his chin. Many explanations have been offered. One is that this magical orb is representing the moon, and the dragon's ability to carry it is a symbol of great power. Another theory is that the pearl is the sun and the dragon is trying to swallow it. He will never succeed.

A Chinese dictionary, *Pan Tsao Kang Mu*, compiled about 1600 A.D. has a full account of the idiosyncracies of the dragon. He is described as being fond of beautiful gems, jade, and swallow's flesh. He is also described as despising iron, the Pride of India or the Azedarac tree, centipedes, and silk dyed in five different colors. When rain is needed a swallow should be offered; when floods are to be restrained, then iron should be displayed. Dragons are born from eggs and they are not immortal.

The dragons of the east have as much wealth as the dragons of the west, but unlike their western counterparts they have the disposition to enjoy it. Their riches are often displayed in fabulous undersea palaces, and should a mortal visit such a place he would come away richer; he would be bearing gold, jewelry, or a unique treasure. Dragons also had magic garments and objects they were willing to give away.

Perhaps the most distinctive characteristic of an eastern dragon is its positive association with water. There is a chief dragon who lives in the sky who alone has clouds, winds, rains, and vapors under his control. He can control these elements, sending them to earth, or not as he wishes. As the chief dragon watches over the interests of the earth the Emperor watches over the interests of his people providing them with temporal and spiritual blessings. This is why the Emperor in China sat on a dragon-throne, and he alone was allowed to have the five-clawed dragon embroidered on the royal robes.

Picture Books and Illustrated Texts: Dragons of the East

Bateson-Hill, Margaret. (1996). *Lao Lao of Dragon Mountain*. Illustrated by Francesca Pelizzoli. Chinese text by Manyee Wan. Paper cuts by Sha-Lui Qu. London: De Agosti Editions. The divine character of dragons is illustrated in this story. Lao Lao is an old lady who led a simple life in the foothills of Lung Shan where the Ice Dragon reigned. She became renowned for her intricate paper cut outs. When word of them reached the notice of the greedy emperor, he assigned two soldiers to take her away to a mountain hideout. Locked in a cold, dark room, Lao Lao was ordered to fill a whole chest with diamond cut outs. Angered by this abuse, the Ice Dragon rescues the old lady and takes her away on his back. She now flies the skies with him covering the trees with pink blossoms in the spring, flowers in the summer, and apples and nuts in the fall. Best of all are the snowflakes she drops from her hands.

Hillman, Elizabeth. (1992). *Min-Yo and the Moon Dragon*. Illustrated by John Wallner. Harcourt Brace Jovanovich, Publishers. This original folk tale is set in a time before there were stars. The moon is about to crash into the earth. A sage predicts that such an event can be prevented by the dragon that lives on the orb. Since the moon can be reached only via a fragile cobweb staircase tiny Min-Yo, a maker of silk rope, is found to be the ideal candidate for the journey. She takes with her some vegetables and the traditional gift for a dragon, a diamond. The moon dragon is delighted to have a visitor, pleased with the food but professes no use for the diamond, nor any of the previous ones he'd been given. The pair toss them to the sky, slowing the moon's descent to earth and creating stars!

Lawson, Julie. (1993). *The Dragon's Pearl*. Illustrated by Paul Morin. New York: Clarion Books. During a terrible drought in "the far away days of cloud-breathing dragons, there lived a boy named Xiao Sheng who loved to sing." He happened upon a luminous pearl in the worst of the dry spell that turned out to be magic. It filled the rice jar to the brim, overflowed the oil jar, and kept the money box full. When neighbors attempted to take the pearl away from Xiao Sheng the boy swallowed it. It transformed him into a dragon who breathed and burst clouds thereby breaking the drought. But the rain fell only on the fields of the good people; the robbers were forced to leave their arid land. The grateful villagers looked after Xiao Sheng's mother for the rest of her days. This is a lovely, haunting story with glorious paintings.

Leaf, Margaret. (1987). *Eyes of the Dragon*. Illustrated by Ed Young. New York: Lothrop, Lee & Shepard Books. The wall around the village is finished, but plain, so the magistrate agrees to the dragon king being painted upon it. An artist, Ch'en Jung, consents to the task so long as he can complete it in his own manner. After many days a magnificent painting of a dragon with no eyes is finished. Ch'en sternly advises the haughty magistrate, who insists they be added, against painting them but is ignored. The artist leaves the scene immediately upoin completing his work and for good reason. Once the eyes of the dragon are in place, the beast lifts himself from the wall destroying it completely. Ed Young has captured the mystery and the atmosphere of the story with his soft, powerful pastel illustrations. This story is unusual since this eastern dragon is uncharacteristically aggressive.

Luenn, Nancy. (1982). *The Dragon Kite*. Illustrated by Michael Hague. New York: Harcourt, Brace, Jovanovich, Inc. *The Dragon Kite* is based on an historical figure, Ishikawa, a much loved Japanese equivalent of Robin Hood. The story opens with the hero contemplating some booty that has thus far eluded him, a pair of golden dolphins that sit atop the castle of the Shogun's son. When Ishikawa sees a kite dancing in the sky, he is struck by a possibility for lifting the treasures. Execution of his plan involves him in being apprenticed to a famous kitemaker for a disciplined four year period. Finally, a dragon kite capable of carrying Ishikawa to the statues and back again is completed. The thief/hero is betrayed by a friend, and he and his family are slated for execution. Unexpectedly they are rescued in time, making for a dramatic ending to the story.

Patterson, Darcy. (1991). *The River Dragon*. Illustrated by Jean & Mou-Sien Tseng. New York: Lothrop, Lee & Shepard Books. Patterson has created an original folk tale out of the lore that surrounds the eastern dragon. Ying Shoo is looked upon with disfavor by his future father-in-law. When the wily father of the bride can no longert put off the customary three feasts that celebrate the coming wedding, he tries to trick the groom. Knowing Ying Shoo has to cross a river in which a dragon lives and knowing the dragon's love of swallows, the bride's father serves the birds at each banquet. When the river dragon smells the birds inside of Ying Shoo, he comes seeking them as offering. The groom has has no choice but to scare the monster away. This he does with a centipede and a five colored scarf, items that are anathemas to dragons. But, on the third attempt at crossing the river Ying Shoo has only his wits. Fortunately they serve him well and he and his bride live happily every after.

Troughton, Joanna. (1995). *Monkey and the Water Dragon*. Illustrated by the author. London: Dutton. This story of an amazing journey was first written in the sixteenth century in China by Wu Ch'eng-en. The goddess Kuan-Yin chooses the gentle scholar Tripitaka to carry some Buddhist scriptures from India to China. Two servants with magical powers are provided to protect him—a monkey who is somewhat mischievous and a lazy pig. *Monkey and the Water Dragon* is a story of one of the adventures the threesome had during this trip. It is the tale of how an evil water dragon who wishes to eat two children is thwarted by Monkey.

Williams, Jay. (1976). *Everyone Knows What a Dragon Looks Like*. Illustrated by Mercer Mayer. New York: Four Winds Press. Han, a cheerful, courteous orphan is the gate-sweeper and savior of the mountainous city of Wu. A message Han brings to the ruling Mandarin and his four counselors panics them with news of the approach of the Wild Horseman of the North. The rulers decide their best hope is to appeal to the Great Cloud Dragon for help. When a little fat, bald man arrives at the gate claiming to be the dragon to whom the city prayed, no one except Han believes him. Only because the little boy treats the man with respect does he transform to a "real" dragon and turn back the marauding attackers with a great wind. Han immediately becomes a hero in the city!

Yep, Laurence. (1995). *The City of Dragons*. Illustrated by Jean and Mou-Sien Tseng. New York: Scholastic, Inc. This is a modern folk tale set in once upon a time land. It revolves around a little boy who has the saddest face in the whole world and is an embarrassment to the village. He runs away ashamed encountering some giants in a caravan on their way to the city of dragons beneath the sea. They take the child with them. His sad face encourages the dragon maidens to cry, and the tears they produce are wondrous shiny pearls. The giants are delighted and return the boy back to his village with some of the stones. It is now the turn of the people to be ashamed of the way they acted; and they welcome him home as a hero, never tiring of listening to his adventures.

Yep, Laurence. (1994). *The Junior Thunder Lord*. Illustrated by Robert Van Nutt. Bridgewater Books. The sentiment that those at the top should help those at the bottom is skillfully woven throughout Laurence Yep's lusty retelling of a seventeenth century Chinese fable. Yue, a merchant, alone of all people in a drought stricken land helps a strange, huge, hairy creature. In time, the giant known to all as Bear Face, is able to help Yue in more ways than could be imagined. First, Bear Face saves Yue from drowning; and then when he reveals his true identity as a junior thunder lord, he squeezes a rain cloud to relieve the drought over Yue's home.

Miscellaneous Books: Dragons

Some of these texts feature contemporary dragons which tend to resemble their folklore ancestors but often not their characteristics.

Base, Graeme. (1996). *The Discovery of Dragons*. Illustrated by the author. Melbourne, Australia: Harry N. Abrams, Inc., Publishers. Base's fertile imagination and wondrous artistic talents have been put to use in this lively speculation on how dragons were actually located in the world. Base's thesis, presented under the personage of Rowland W. Greasebeam, (B.Sc.) is that individuals discovered different kinds of dragons at different times. Around the middle of the ninth century a Viking warrior by name of Bjørn of Brømme while out pillaging, looting, and engaging in gratuitous violence discovered the European dragon. Similarly, Soong Mei Ying in letters to her Venerable Father around 1277 describes the Asiatic dragons she stumbles upon. Last, Dr. E. F. Liebermann in epistles to his long suffering fiancee makes note of the Tropical dragons. The final correspondence takes place in and around the 1850s. This text is immensely entertaining!

Baskin, Hosie and Leonard. (1985). *A Book of Dragons*. Illustrated by the Leonard Baskin. New York: Alfred A. Knopf. The Baskins have collaborated on a text that describes 22 dragons from different mythologies and from literature around the world. The most famous of all western dragons, that slain by St. George, is featured as are many other lesser known creatures such as the malignant, bird-like monster demanding all the food of the people of Wavel, leaving them to starve. Most of the dragons are malicious for some reason; they are guarding their treasure or are under enchantment. But there is an almost winsome "monster" described called the Fold-Up Dragon. It survives on leavings of other dragons, mostly hiding and sleeping. Because this particular dragon is so retiring few legends are known about it! The Baskins' text is an interesting one for whetting a reader's appetite to know more about these strange creatures.

LeGuin, Ursula. (1989). *Fire and Stone*. Illustrated by Laura Marshall. New York: Atheneum. Out of the north the dragon would fly, screeching its "dreadful, hungry cry—RRRAAAHHHX! RRRAAAHHHX!" The people of the village, warned by the ringing village bells would hide in Rocky Pond and quiver. Once a little girl and a little boy of the town, Min and Podo, decided to take the monster at its word and threw it some rocks. "The dragon was as quick as a barn swallow catching gnats." And twice as greedy. He refused no offering of a rock from the villagers finally eating so many he could not fly. He finally turned to stone, "all its fire and hunger" gone. Nowadays Dragon Hill is a good place to watch the sunrise.

Mahy, Margaret. (1992). *The Dragon of an Ordinary Family.* Illustrated by Helen Oxenbury. New York: Dial Books for Young Readers. The cheap baby dragon Mr. Belsaki brought home as an "I'll show you," pet for son, Orlando, on the day Mrs. Belsaki called him a "fuddy-duddy" turns the ordinary life of the family into an extraordinary one. When the dragon's size and breath make it difficult to keep him in the yard, he surprises the family with a vacation to the Isles of Magic "the homes of all the wonderful, strange, fairy-tale people." There the Belsakis see dark old forests, starry castles, princesses and meet all kinds of sons—"the youngest sons of kings, of millers, of cobblers, and of beggars—all seeking fortunes." The story is full of surprises to the end!

Munsch, Robert. N. (1980). *The Paper Bag Princess.* Illustrated by Michael Martchenko. New York: Ashton Scholastic. Muncsh's tale is a charming twist on the conventional fairy tale of dragons, maidens, and princes. The dragon who smashes down Princess Elizabeth's castle, burns all her clothes with his fiery breath, and carries off her intended, Prince Ronald, does the young lady a great favor. Reduced to wearing only a paper bag, the feisty maiden tracks down the beast and tricks it in a humorous exchange into allowing her into his cave. Far from being grateful to be rescued, Ronald reveals his true shallow nature when he tells Elizabeth "Come back when you are dressed like a real princess." Elizabeth then explains she will not bother at all!

Robinson, Fay. (1996). *Where Did All the Dragons Go?* Illustrated by Victor Lee. Bridgewater Books. "Long ago and by and by, dragons ruled the earth and sky." The rhyming words of this text are accompanied by gloriously fanciful illustrations of dragons hanging upside down from trees, cavorting in water and clouds, playing fiery games. While the adults were frightened of the dragons the children always knew that "dragons, in their hearts, were good." But one starry autumn night the dragon leader boomed across the heavens, "Now's the time." All knew what to do—the beating of the dragon wings filled the sky as they flew off. The children sadly wondered why the large creatures called a sad good-bye at the edge of earth and sky. "That's the last t'was ever heard of dragons—not another word." But who knows, they might be waiting yet!

Sutcliff, Rosemary. (1993). *The Minstrel and the Dragon Pup.* Illustrated by Emma Chichester Clark. Cambridge, MA: Candlewick Press. By chance a poor minstrel is present at the hatching of a dinosaur egg and he sings the little creature a lullaby, "a tune for waking up to." The pup responds to the music as he does to the kind ministrations of the musician. Together they take up a life together, happy and content on the road until a thief lures "Lucky" away. Once more by chance the minstrel is united with the now miserable dragon pup, again by virtue of his lovely haunting tune. This contemporary and rather lengthy story has a feel of folklore and a quality of timelessness about it.

Water Beings

Water beings of folk lore are many, but material for younger readers, particularly in picture book format, tends to be limited to mermaids and selchies both of which are discussed below.

Mermaids

Mermaids (and their less well known counterpart, mermen) are marine creatures that are half woman (or men) and half fish; the top being a human form and the bottom a fish tail. Their being could be attributed to sailors accounts of the dugong, an herbivorous aquatic mammal that frequents warm coastal waters of the far east where they can be observed basking on the surface of the water. From a distance these animals have a head that is a rude approach to a human outline. In addition, they are immensely affectionate and the mother will suckle her young by holding it with her flipper to one of two pectoral teats. If she is disturbed for any reason the female will suddenly dive underwater and flip up her fish-like tail.

The mermaid is traditionally famed for her beauty and her beautiful palaces under the water. She has an uncanny ability to sing, her magic voice being so dulcet and harmonious as to calm the roughest sea. She can also use this power to lure men to their death. Because sailors are so enchanted by the beauty of the sound, they are seduced into allowing their ships too close to the rocks and become shipwrecked. On occasion they drown. Then the mermaid is known as a siren. The classic mermaid, like the fairy, also is enamored of dancing and would dance either in the sea or on land as a human.

But, the mermaid or merman is not always a creature to be envied despite great beauty. The story of Glaucus and Scylla of Greek mythology is a case in point. Glaucus was a fisherman who inexplicably becomes changed to a creature of the sea with trailing sea-green hair, broad shoulders, and a fish tail. He became entranced with a beautiful maiden, Scylla, who, alas, would have none of his overtures or entreaties. Forlorn and heartsick Glaucus sought the counsel of the enchantress Circe. As she herself was in love with the merman, the witch took great pleasure in exacting an intolerable price for the spurned Glaucus. Using magic potions and charms which she spread around the bay in Sicily where Scylla lived and swam, Circe changed the girl's limbs into a brood of serpents from which she could not escape. Scylla's disposition grew as ugly as her body and she remained where she was, rooted to the ground. Her favorite sport was to devour mariners who came within reach! The mighty Ulysses lost six companions to the monster. Scylla eventually became a rock.

A similarly poignant story of doomed characters is told by Hans Christian Andersen in *The Little Mermaid*. In this tale the mermaid cannot hope for salvation because she does not have a soul. This she cannot attain unless she marries a human who is in love with her. Sadly, the prince for whom she sacrifices all marries someone else. But all is not lost for the little mermaid whose thorough selflessness brings her a certain reward.

There are not many stories about mermaids or mermen available in the picture book format. One exception is Andersen's *Little Mermaid*. Only two versions are reviewed below.

Mermaid Stories: Picture Books and Illustrated Texts

Andersen, Hans Christian (1993). *The Little Mermaid*. Illustrated by Charles Santore. New York: Jelly Bean Press. This famous poignant story as first published in 1837, is used in this text. Santore has illustrated this tale in dramatic and extravagant fashion adding greatly to the majesty and the wonder of the story. The various changes of moods are subtly expressed in different shades of color. The detail of the mermaids, the prince, and their respective worlds, is astonishing and lifelike. It never occurs to the reader that the life under the sea is only a fantasy.

Isadora, Rachel. (1998). *The Little Mermaid*. Illustrated by Rachel Isadora. New York: G. P. Putnam's Sons. Isadora has managed to reduce the story of the young mermaid to its essence without losing the drama of the tale. Much of the tale is carried by the watercolor illustrations that are bathed in blues and browns. The moods are variously joyous, frightening, eerie, and sad and are powerfully conveyed visually. Particularly compelling is the ending when the little mermaid is allowed to join the children of air. As she floats above the water for the first time in her life "she felt joy."

McHargue, Georgess. (1973). *The Mermaid and the Whale*. Illustrated by Robert Andrew Parker. New York: Holt, Rinehart and Winston, Inc. An author's note states that this story was a sailor's yarn, popular on Cape Cod more than a century ago. A mermaid who lived off of Sandwich Town, in Massachusetts's whaling days, falls in love with Long John, a fine, canny, and fast whale. Her infatuation with him is complete and shameless. The mermaid uses every ploy she can to have the giant mammal notice her, to no avail. When the battle of wits appears to be in the sea woman's favor, Long John manages simultaneously to dispatch the tenacious creature and rid himself of the seaweed harness into which he was fitted. "Even today, great kelpy ropes of it wash up on the shore near Sandwich, so that anyone who wants to can own a piece of the Mermaid's bridle."

San Souci, Robert D. (1997). *Nicolas Pipe*. Illustrated by David Shannon. New York: Dial Books for Young Readers. *Nicolas Pipe* was a merman. "Beneath the waves he would swim for hours with his powerful fishtail, but when he left the sea, he walked on two legs like any other man." He could do this by the good offices of a sorcerer whose child he had once rescued from drowning. Nicolas was loved by a beautiful maiden by name of Margaret. He loved her in return but as he was of the sea and she of the land, they had many difficulties to overcome before they could wed. San Souci has based this story on an account of an English priest (c. 1140-1208) who was renowned for his wit and his storytelling ability in the court of Henry II.

San Souci, Robert, D. (1992). *Sukey and the Mermaid*. Illustrated by Brian Pinkney. New York: Four Winds Press. Until recently reports of the mermaid in the African-American culture were rare. Those stories that are being told are thought to have been brought to North America by black Portuguese immigrants from communities of the Cape Verde Islands off the African coast. Robert D. San Souci has retold one of the more well known African-American tales, *Sukey and the Mermaid.* A little girl, Sukey, is bowed down by the demands made on her by her stepfather she calls "Mister Hard-Times." When she sneaks a respite at the sea from him one hot day, she unwittingly calls up "Mama Jo," a beautiful, brown-skinned, black-eyed mermaid. The sea woman becomes a benevolent protector to Sukey, guiding her through her maturity and marriage and the process of getting rid of "Mister Hard-Times."

Osborne, Mary Pope. (1993). *Mermaid Tales From Around the World*. Illustrated by Troy Howell. New York: Scholastic, Inc. Osborne has elegantly retold stories about mermaids (and a mermen) from 12 different countries. In the west, and in the one African story related, *The Sea Husband,* the relationship between mortal and mermaid tends to be a doomed one. The sea creature and lover are typically unable to sustain their relationship. The eastern perspective tends to be more positive. Mortals usually benefit over their lifetime if they extend a kindness to any creature of the deep.

Selchies
Among the more poignant of sea stories are those about selkies or selchies. These are seals who take on a human form to dance or celebrate an event on land. In order to do this they have to shed their skin. If this skin is carelessly discarded or found by a human, then the water creature has no choice but to remain on land. The stories around these events are always bittersweet. While the creatures, who are both male and female, have the form of a person, they are always true to the sea. When the skin is located again, the selchie will don it and return to his or her roots in the waves. This the animals will do even if the interval on land has been considerable and enjoyable.

Most of the stories about selchies come from the Orkney and Shetland Islands and in coastal areas of Scotland. Selchies are not unknown in Ireland and Scandinavia as well. Gentle, air-breathing creatures, they dwell in deep underwater caverns and have been known to take humans such as seal hunters down to them to shame them into giving up their trade.

Picture Books: Selchie Stories

Cooper, Susan. (1986). *The Selkie Girl*. Illustrated by Warwick Hutton. New York: A Margaret K. Elderry Book. Donallan, a lonely farmer on an isolated island, is warned by wise Old Thomas that the singing girl he sighted and loved on the beach is a selkie. She is a seal and sheds her skin to take on the form of a woman once a year. Old Thomas warns she can be captured but "a wild creature will always go back to the wild." And so it came to pass. Mairi was taken as Donallan's bride and bore him five children, all of which she loved dearly. But the call of the sea and her seal children was too strong and she returned to it. From her watery home she protected them all; when Donallan went fishing he caught many fish, when it was stormy his boat was always safe. Even today can be heard a selkie song on the wind blowing around Donallan's house.

Gerstein, Mordicai. (1986). *The Seal Mother*. Illustrated by the author. New York: Dial Books for Young Readers. The story is a variant of the tale about a seal woman, a selkie, who is brought forcibly to land by a lovesick suitor. While she remains loyal and loving as a wife and mother she longs always to return to the sea. Eventually this happens. In this iteration Andrew, the boy of the marriage between the selkie and the fisherman, maintains a close association with his mother and her family. At Midsummer's Eve, particularly, they meet on a tiny rock island in the sea and dance, laugh, and sing all night long. There is an interesting twist to the end of this version that piques the imagination of the reader.

MacGill-Callahan, Sheila. (1995). *The Seal Prince*. Illustrated by Kris Waldherr. New York: Dial Books for Young Readers. "In the days that were, a daughter was born to the lord and lady of Skye to comfort them in their old age. They called her Grainne, which means Grace." Little Grainne grew to be good so it was in her nature to rescue a trapped baby seal on her eighth birthday. Every year on the same day Grainne went back to that rock and every year the growing seal visited her. But when she was eighteen there was a young man to greet her in the seal's place. His name was Deodatus and he was in love with the gracious Grainne. How these two of different worlds solved the dilemma posed by their affection for one another is a moving story. This is an old tale with many versions.

Yolen, Jane. (1968, 1991). *Greyling*. Illustrated by David Ray. New York: Philomel Books. A fisherman and his wife longed for a child, "But year in and year out the cradle stayed empty." One day the fisherman carried home a baby seal he found crying on a sandbar. Upon opening the shirt wrapping the couple found a strange child, one with grey hair and grey eyes. He was a selchie, a man on land and a seal in the water. The wife named him *Greyling*, raised him as her own, never allowing him to enter the sea. For his part *Greyling* grieved for what he did not know. But the call of the water was too great for the seal/boy during a storm when the fisherman was drowning at sea. *Greyling* dove into the turbulent turf rescuing his father and finding his roots in the process.

Fairies

The term fairy is derived from the Latin *fatum* which means fate, destiny, or possessing magical powers. Certainly these mysterious beings use their power in various ways, mischievously, vindictively, or to work good in the world of the human.

Fairies exist in every culture; they feature especially large in Celtic stories from Ireland, Scotland, England, and Wales but appear less frequently in African American tales.

The origin of western fairies is a source of dispute among scholars. One widely told story from the West Highlands in Scotland relates that fairies once lived in Heaven as angels. They lived in harmony with God. But about the time He was creating the universe it happened that one of their number, the Proud Angel, introduced a spirit of discontent which influenced the foolish among them. The angels began to oppose God. They became rebellious with dark thoughts and even began to take up a matching dark appearance. God was patient with these foolish beings but in the end was forced to part the curtains of mist that enveloped the Heavens and contemplate their fate. He decided to send them off into the dark blackness that existed beyond. In the midst of the darkness was a terrible red light that gleamed like a fire.

When God sent off the rebellious one and the followers to this pool of black, telling them there was no room for them in Heaven, the Proud Angel left with a parting shot that not all the angels left were good.

"Some," he said, "were not against God but they were not for him either. They were neutral."

Indeed it proved to be so. God was later forced to confront these neutrals, telling them He could not keep them with the good angels any longer. His decision was to send the angels down, beyond the curtains of Heaven to earth where they could live underground in the hills and come out only at night. He told them that the people of the earth would call them fairies.

There are other stories about the origin of fairies that are enchanting. In Cornwall, England, an old superstition exists that they are the ancient Druids or religious leaders of the ancient Celtic people. When they refused to convert to Christianity from their pagan faith they became smaller and smaller and smaller.

In the west the image of a fairy as a dainty creature with gauze wings is prevalent. It was not always so. Prior to the influence of Shakespeare and the Victorian era, fairies were thought to be as large as people and of both sexes. The bard of Avon was to suggest their diminutive form which has persisted as an image when he wrote in *Midsummer Night's Dream:*

> *Fairies small, two feet tall,*
> *With caps of red upon their heads.*

World of Fairy on Earth

As noted above fairies live in hills in the earth, at least in the western tradition. The entrance to fairy land is to be found by a number of means—by penetrating a sepulchral mound, by passing through a cave, fading into a cleft in a rock, or down in a well. The mortal who makes it through to the fairy kingdom is likely to be surprised at the beauty of the land beneath; the landscape will be pleasant and restful and the caverns will likely be filled with rich stones and sparkling jewelry. Once in this wondrous underworld the human must not eat anything, for if he tastes fairy food he will be a captive for all time.

Like their land, the race itself is beautiful. The appearance of a fairy is of an arresting nature that transfixes mere mortals who encounter the fey in their usual occupations of dancing, singing, or horse riding. This happens in spite of any fears harbored by a person about being in their company.

There are a number of interesting aspects of fairy life. As suggested by Shakespeare's verse, red (along with white and green) are the colors of the clothes and adornments worn by fairy-folk. Certain flowers are associated with fairies. During a thunderstorm they will take shelter under the leaves of the primrose flower. Eating calendulas was reputed to make one see fairies, but picking a foxglove would make them angry and the fairy may steal your child in retaliation. Another aspect of fairy life that recurs in stories frequently is a disregard for time. Humans who spend time in the underworld, or even just time with fairies, are usually startled at their release to discover they have been away from their loved ones for a period of years. They think it has been days.

Seldom do fairies have names but rather are thought of as collective beings. Certainly in the superstitious Europe of the past, to mention a fairy name was not permissible. A primitive belief existed that the name of a person is implicitly part of the individual and to know this name presupposes a certain measure of power over him or her. This superstition seemed to apply more particularly in the case of supernatural beings. Indeed the magic power of a name is a motif in many fairy tales.

Neither was it considered good practice by folk, at least in the times of the sixteenth and seventeenth century to refer to them as fallen angels. The imputation that they are evil spirits caused them to be outraged and dangerous. In addition, fairies dislike the commonly understood term preferring instead to be known by such terms as "Wee Folk," "Good Folk," or "Good Neighbors."

Sometime fairies are true to such names as "Good Neighbors" and they help those dispossessed or helpless in some fashion. The Welsh "Tylwyth Teg" rescue Huw, as far as they are able, from the morose and at times cruel attentions of his farmer father in a story told by Susan Cooper called *The Silver Cow*. Further, they are known as generous benefactors willing to provide gold and jewels to those so favored or to those that have been kind to them. Some fairies, bestow gifts that are less tangible but more valuable. Ability to play a musical instrument and to pass this skill to descendants is one of the commonest. In Scandinavia the Näck or Fossegrim who dwells in a waterfall will teach humans his musical art.

Perhaps the most enchanting of all beliefs that surround fairies is the understanding by an American or British child that if he or she leaves a shedded milk tooth under the pillow the tooth fairy will pay for it. No one knows how common this custom was, since it is rarely mentioned in folk tale collections and it is not one observed in Europe. (In that continent the donor of the coins is said to be a mouse.) Tom Paxton has contributed an original fairy tale he has named *The Story of the Tooth Fairy* that accounts for this custom which the author notes is a token of friendship between the fey and mortals.

But sometimes the fairies can be exceedingly cruel. They will snatch human babies away and leave a fairy child in its place instead. These switched babies are called changelings—creatures that look very young but are, in fact, quite ancient. If a mother believes she is subject to this action she has to do something to make the changeling laugh to break the spell. A typical response was to carry out a bizarre act such as boiling water in egg shells. Antonia Barber has used this fairy deceit as the basis for her original folk tale *Catkin*.

Like their cousins to the south, the fairies of Norse mythology also live underground but they were variously called trolls or elves. Danish tradition avers that on certain nights those hills under which trolls live rise up on pillars of gold. It is possible to watch the trolls at their merriment, particularly their feasting. Some trolls were white and others were black. The latter studiously avoided the light as a mortal enemy since it would turn them into stones. They were noted for their knowledge of nature and as skilled artisans making many wondrous things out of wood and metal. It was the black elves who made the famous hammer used by Thor, the Norse god, that always returned to him.

Picture Books and Illustrated Texts: World of Fairy on Earth
Barber, Antonia. (1994). *Catkin*. Illustrated by P. J. Lynch. Cambridge, MA: Candlewick Press. The Little People who live in the hill leave a changeling for baby Carrie, the much loved baby daughter of the farmer and his wife. It is up to *Catkin*, a tiny, ginger kitten to retrieve the child from the immortal world to which she has been taken. This he does with great wit, courage, and compassion answering truthfully all the riddles posed him. But answering truthfully poses a fourth riddle which no one but the wise old woman at the top of the hill can resolve.

Cooper, Susan. (1983). *The Silver Cow*. Illustrated by Warwick Hutton. New York: Atheneum. In the green hills of Wales is a lake, Llyn Barfog, in English "the bearded lake." *The Silver Cow* is the story of how this came to be. Huw, son of a morose farmer and poorly treated, watches cows every day. He plays his harp up the mountain by the lake where the cows graze. One day a strange shining cow emerged, joined the herd and gave rich milk. So did her progeny. Soon the farmer was wealthy, but grew greedy and would not heed Huw's warnings that the cow was sent by the "Tylwyth Teg." Sure enough when the cow was due to be slaughtered she disappeared with her offspring into the lake. Broad, white water lilies floated on the water where the cows had disappeared, giving rise to the name by which the lake is known.

Forest, Heather. (1990). *The Woman Who Flummoxed the Fairies*. Illustrated by Susan Gaber. San Diego: Harcourt Brace Jovanovich, Publishers. The fairies longed for a taste of the delicious cakes made by the baker woman. All they had ever feasted on were leftover crumbs since the cakes were always eaten to the last bite. In frustration the fairies kidnaped the woman taking her down to their underworld kingdom. Now the clever cook knew that if she baked a cake for them down in the evermore world she would never see her husband and babe again. So she confuses or flummoxes the good folk with a series of tricks, the end result of which is her return to her forest cottage. But she does honor her promise to the little people that she would make them a cake. She knows they accepted her gift for they left her some fairy gold in its place.

Macdonald, George. (1987). *Little Daylight*. Adapted by Anthea Bell. Illustrated by Dorothée Duntz. New York: North-South Books. The little girl born to the delighted king and queen was called Daylight because of her bright shiny eyes. Five of the fairies who lived in the nearby woods blessed the child with "such gifts as each counted best" but an old wicked thing whom some thought a witch, cursed her. "She shall sleep all day, if Daylight be her name and wax and wane with the moon." A sixth and seventh fairy undid as much of the curse as possible but still the girl was under enchantment until she was kissed unknowingly by a prince. Indeed it came to pass in a most delightful fashion and in the face of the continuing spite of the wicked fairy.

MacDonald, Margaret Read. (1997). *Slop*. Illustrated by Yvonne LeBrun Davis. Goldon, Colorado: Fulcrum Publishing. Nightly the old man empties the heavy slop bucket full of onion peels, potato skins, and dish water over the front fence until he is startled by a little voice, "I wish you would stop doing that." When the owner of the voice, a fairy man, and the old man touch feet the fairy home is revealed. There it is covered in peelings and scraps! What a mess! What a conundrum for the old man and the old woman! The pair solve the difficulty of disposing of their garbage without too much difficulty and find their lives enriched more than they could have imagined. This Welsh folk tale has characteristic motifs in the illustrations—a corgi dog (which the wee folk ride!), leeks, and a Welsh vole. This is a charming little tale for young children.

Munsch, Robert. (1998). *Andrew's Loose Tooth*. Illustrated by Michael Martchenko. Ontario, Canada: Scholastic. "When Andrew came downstairs, there were three big, red apples in the middle of the table. Even though he had a loose tooth, he decided to eat an apple." That was his undoing and the start of a very funny story. Noone, not mother, father, nor the dentist with a tooth on his car (and a suspect mode of operation), could extract the tooth. But, friend Louis knew what to do. He called the Tooth Fairy who roared up right away on her motorcycle! Even she was defeated! "Incredible," said the Tooth Fairy. "This is the first tooth ever that I can't pull out." Needless to say the tooth came out eventually and the said fairy got her tooth albeit in a somewhat unconventional fashion!

Paxton, Tom. (1996). *The Story of the Tooth Fairy*. Illustrated by Robert Sauber. New York: Morrow Junior Books. When seven year old Emily playing in the garden happens unexpectedly upon fairy Glynnis, they become friends. The Fairy Queen is excited by Glynnis' report of her encounter with the child since there had been no contact with mortals for years. Glynnis was asked to visit Emily and to bring back something only a mortal could give as a sign that the time was right to renew the friendship. Glynnis returned with her friend's tooth that had fallen out. In exchange she left her some fairy money under her pillow! And the custom continues. The sharing of milk teeth is now a symbol of the friendship between the fey and mortals.

White, Carolyn. (1997). *Whuppity Stoorie*. Illustrated by S. D. Schindler. New York: G. P. Putnam's Sons. The lady in green who whirled in and promised to cure Kate of Kittlerumpit's pig seemed like an answer to a prayer for the girl and her mother. But it was not so. The swirling lady drove a hard bargain—her price for her "good works" was to take Kate to fairy land and to claim her as one of the fey. But in accordance with fairy law, the green lady could claim her bounty only after three days. She could not claim the child at all if her name became known. By chance Kate discovered it to be *Whuppity Stoorie* and in the nick of time was able to save herself an unhappy fate. In addition, she was able to spend many happy days entertaining the pig, Grumphie and her three babies. *Whuppity Stoorie* became history!

Yolen, Jane. (1990). *Tam Lin*. Illustrated by Charles Mikolaycak. San Diego: Harcourt Brace Jovanovich, Publishers. "Jennet MacKenzie, who had skin the color of new cream and hair the red-gold of a sunrise" set about to reclaim her inheritance, Cauterhaugh, from the fairies when she turned 16. Cauterhaugh was a "forbidding castle, with ruined towers on a weedy piece of land," and one red rose. Jennet pulled the flower and by so doing summoned a handsome young man, *Tam Lin*, from the land of Ever-Fair. He told Jennet how to bring him back from the clutches of the fairy folk. She followed his fearful directions and won herself a husband in addition to her birthright. This version of *Tam Lin*, which is lengthy, is based on an ancient Scottish ballad.

World of Fairy on the Mountain

The fairies of the east frequently live in high places, often on the top of mountains, in contrast to their western cousins whose abode is underground. They are also mischievous and not above interfering with the lives of mortals, although their intent is generally not malevolent.

One particularly lovely story where fairy interference is the centerpiece of the tale is available in three different retellings of an ancient Chinese legend in picture book format—Demi's *The Magic Tapestry*, Marilee Heyer's *The Weaving of a Dream*, and Robert D. San Souci's *The Enchanted Tapestry*. A widow with three sons devotes much time to weaving a heavenly tapestry which is whisked away by fairies upon completion. The mother almost fades away from grief and the sons seek the return of the work. Only the youngest of the three boys is willing to pay the heavy price asked and undergo the required adventures. However, he not only retrieves the valued work but wins himself a bride from among the fairy folk. All three books are rather lengthy and would appeal to older children.

This love by fairies of beautiful cloth is again evident in a story by Ellin Greene she has called *Ling-Li and the Phoenix Fairy*. The story features Ling-Li and Manchang a couple who were poor, industrious, thrifty, and very much in love. When they decided to marry Ling-Li spun the thread, wove the cloth, and embroidered her wedding dress. For three whole months she worked and the gown she eventually made was gorgeous. But then it was stolen, first by a spoilt villager and then by magpies. Ling-Li set out to get it back. She tracked the garment down to the phoenix fairy who returned it upon request and gave her blessing to the marriage. The troubles of the couple were not over after the wedding, but Ling-Li was to continue to be blessed by the Phoenix Fairy.

The Phoenix Fairy in Ellen Greene's story is both supernatural being and Queen of the Birds. She changes from a spirit maiden after she greets Ling-Li to a glorious bird depicted as part pheasant, part peacock, and part bird of paradise. The Phoenix is old in Chinese mythology. It differs from the Greek understanding of the bird and is considered as representing the female or *yin* principle.

The Japanese have an enchanting fairy called Chin-Chin Kobakama who is in charge of the thick mats that often covered the floors of a Japanese home. If the inhabitants of the house fail to keep these mats clean the fairies will tease them. Such a teasing takes place in the story by Robin Palmer in her text *Fairy Elves*. The charming and pretty Kiyoko was petted and spoiled by servants until she married. Her husband's family did not have the same number of servants and she was expected to pick up after herself more than she was used to. When her husband was away Kiyoko was awakened at the hour of the ox, about two o'clock in the morning, by hundreds of tiny men dancing about her, brandishing their swords, and laughing at the bride. The same thing happened the next night and the next. Soon Kiyoko was frightened to sleep. The girl looked wan and pale. Her appearance frightened her husband on his return and he begged of his wife to explain what was the matter. He took charge of the problem by throwing a sword into the midst of the gathering the next night and all the little, dancing men disappeared. In fact, they turned into toothpicks! It seems that Kiyoko had been too lazy to discard properly the toothpick she had used after the evening meal and she had merely poked it into the mat. Shamed by the fairies she never did it again!

Texts Cited

Demi. (1994). *The Magic Tapestry*. Illustrated by the author. New York: Henry Holt and Company.

Greene, E. (1996). *Ling-Li and the Phoenix Fairy*. Illustrated by Zong-Zhou Wang. New York: Clarion Books.

Heyer, M. (1986). *The Weaving of a Dream*. Illustrated by the author. New York: Viking Kestral.

Palmer, R. (1964). *Fairy Elves*. New York: H. Z. Walck.

San Souci, D. R. (1987). *The Enchanted Tapestry*. Illustrated by László Gál. London: Methueun Children's Books.

4

Trickster Folk Tales

The Trickster

The trickster is a significant character who is part of all cultures but appears in different forms and answers to many names. He is an individual, god, or animal who uses wit and frequently magical ability to change form to triumph over creatures who are more powerful than himself.

The trickster is immensely complex and contradictory. Sometimes he is noble, compassionate, and a hero; other times he is ignoble, greedy, and the author of considerable mischief. Frequently, he can be all of the above in the same story. In short, the trickster is representative of the best and worst in man and perhaps nature. To the Native American the trickster sometimes represented the vagaries of the environment, sometimes gentle and forgiving and sometimes malevolent.

Many societies regarded the trickster character with reverence. He was the hope of the American slaves, for instance, as they fought a cruel system. Slaves could identify with the relatively weak but feisty character who could overcome long odds to succeed. Moreover, the trickster is sometimes regarded as being the creator of the world and the provider of many elements needed by man such as fire and light. This is true in both African and Native American cultures where the trickster sometimes assumes the status of a deity.

In as much as the character of the trickster is universal, the same can be said for some of the stories. One of the most widely told is the crop division tale. Janet Stevens has a lively version called *Tops and Bottoms* with Hare and Bear as the antagonists. The two become business partners. Hare works the land Bear owns and they split the crops grown, tops and bottoms. When Bear picks tops, Hare grows carrots; when Bear picks bottoms, Hare grows lettuce and broccoli. When Bear picks tops and bottoms, Hare grows corn and delivers the roots and tassels to his neighbor. Enraged, Bear declares their partnership dissolved and determines to plant his own crops from now on.

The actors differ but the story is the same all around the world. The German Grimm brothers have a version called *The Peasant and the Devil* in which the adversaries are a cunning farmer and the prince of lies. The crops are parsnips and grain. A peasant outwits a bear in the Russian iteration of the tale, and in Egypt the characters are wolf and mouse. In Communist China the farmer tricks his greedy landlord. Every culture seems to treasure the cunning of the underdog.

Another universal trickster story is that of outdoing the ingrate. A creature of a wild and untrustworthy disposition, such as a tiger, is trapped in some fashion and appeals to another for help. The helper allows the pitiful nature of the situation to overcome his natural caution, frees the creature, is then himself captured and in danger from the creature he just released. The situation is resolved by a third party, a trickster of some kind. Tololwa M. Mollel has used this story line adroitly in *Shadow Dance*. The crocodile rescued by the cheerful little girl, Salome, turns upon her threatening to make

Figure 2: The Trickster

Country/Ethnic Group	Name of Trickster
Africa - East	Hare
Africa - West	Anansi the Spider
England	Jack
Europe	Reynard the Fox
Cambodia	Rabbit
Holland	Tyl Uilenspiegel
Nigeria	Tortoise
Norway	Loki
United States	
African-American	High John the Conqueror
	Brer Rabbit
Appalachia	Aunt Nancy
	Jack
Indian: Pacific Northwest	Raven
Indian: West	Coyote
Indian: Plains	Iktomi
Indian: Northeast	Mahtoqueh the Hare

the child his supper. The reptile claims he will spare the girl's life if someone can give him a good reason to do so. It looks bleak for Salome when the tree and the cow claim, for their own reasons, no use for little girls in general. It was the pigeon, by pretending not to understand, goads the crocodile into demonstrating how he was placed when Salome found him. Now the ingrate is back to where he started, trapped in a gully. And that is where Salome and the pigeon leave him!

Africa

African folk tales do not embrace the magic that is part of the European tradition. Folk heroes, such as the tricksters, *Anansi the Spider* and *Hare* instead rely on native cunning and reserve to best an opponent. They do not seek the grace or intervention of a supernatural being to help them overcome adversity, nor do they have the ability to shape shift or resurrect themselves if they have been dashed to pieces. In short, the magic of the African folk tale is beating the odds, triumphing over an impossible situation. But, African characters frequently converse and interact with the gods, almost as equals. Certainly they are treated as such if they prove worthy.

Picture Books: African Tricksters

Aardema, Verna. (1997). *Anansi Does the Impossible!* Illustrated by Lisa Desimini. New York: Atheneum Books for Young Readers. Aardema's retelling of this well known tale of how all the stories in the world came to be gains some energy from the fact that Anansi's wife, Aso (AY-so) is really the brains behind Anansi's success. To be sure it is the little spider who has the pluck and daring, but the ideas for bringing off the three impossible tasks asked by the Sky God are firmly his wife's.

Aardema, Verna. (1994). *Oh, Kojo! How Could You!* Illustrated by Marc Brown. New York: Dial Books for Young Readers. Aardema's humorous retelling of this Ashanti story explains in rhythmical language how a cat helps a young chief get the better of Ananse, the trickster, and is revered for his troubles to this day. Born of the spirit of the river, Kojo, a young boy, is able to turn tables on the greedy spider man who tricks him out of three packets of gold dust and a magic ring. Kojo does this with the help of a cat who rescues the stolen ring in the face of significant odds.

Aardema, Verna. (1992). *Anansi Finds a Fool.* Illustrated by Bryna Waldman. New York: Dial Books for Young Readers. Aardema's story has a parallel in Eric A. Kimmel's *Anansi Goes Fishing*, reviewed below. In Aardema's telling the trickster is portrayed as a man, as is sometimes the case, while in Kimmel's version his spider shape is supremely intact. In these tales Anansi wishes for the benefits of fishing without the activity. Forewarned, his fishing companion turns the tables and tricks the spiderman both into doing all the work and out of the fish caught.

Haley, Gail. E. (1970). *A Story A Story*. Illustrated by the author. New York: Atheneum. A long time ago all the stories of the world belonged to Nyame, the Sky God. "He kept them in a golden box next to his royal stool." When Ananse, the spiderman, wanted to buy the Sky God's stories, the Sky God merely laughed. His price was impossible—three terrible or elusive beings. By wit and cunning, old, weak Ananse carefully secured the items asked and brought them up the ladder he had spun to the sky. The astonished and gracious Sky God praised the doughty trickster and when giving up the box proclaimed "my stories belong to Ananse and shall be called 'Spider Stories.'"

Kimmel, Eric. A. (1994). *Anansi and the Talking Melon*. Illustrated by Janet Stevens. New York: Holiday House. Anansi, the Spider, uses his wiles and humor to gain some melon without any physical effort and makes a fool of Elephant in the process. After burrowing himself in the juicy fruit and eating his fill, Anansi cannot get back out of the hole because he is too big. Elephant, wishing to eat the same juicy melon is dissuaded when it starts to "talk." In great excitement the beast rushes the fruit to the king in whose presence the imprisoned Anansi refuses to say a word. Furious the royal breaks the melon providing the spider an opportunity to escape. But he is not yet finished with his trickery!

Kimmel, Eric. A. (1992). *Anansi Goes Fishing*. Illustrated by Janet Stevens. New York: Holiday House. Warthog, the judge, who presides over the Justice Tree in the jungle, does not believe Anansi when he complains that Turtle tricked him into doing all the work when the pair went fishing. He also refuses to believe that Turtle ate all the catch. Anansi's reputation as a lazy trickster preceded him, and Warthog simply could not believe that the angry spider went home without fish and in disgrace. Kimmel has retold one of the many stories about Anansi in lively fashion, and Stevens has created the characters with force and personality making this book an appealing read.

McDermott, Gerald. (1972). *Anansi the Spider*. Illustrated by the author. New York: Henry Holt and Company. McDermott has explored the more mythical aspects of the trickster figure in this text. His particular retelling of this West African Ashanti tale explains why the moon remains in the sky. All of Anansi's six sons were good sons. They each had a special power which they employed to assist their father when he fell into trouble on a journey. To thank them for their devotion, Anansi promised to award the "great globe of light" he found in the forest to the son who rescued him. Since resolution on this issue was impossible, Nyame, "The God of All Things," took the moon and placed it in the sky for everyone to see.

Mollel, Tololwa, M. (1997). *Ananse's Feast*. Illustrated by Andrew Glass. New York: Clarion Books. In *Ananse's Feast* the formidable trickster becomes the victim of his own deceit. Ananse prepares a lavish meal in a time of scarcity with food he had stored on his farm. He is annoyed when Akye, the turtle, drops by on the hopes of getting a bite since he had no intention of sharing. Ananse then proceeds to trick the hapless and hungry Akye out of a meal! Akye, however, is not as slow as he looks and he turns the tables. Mollel is a master storyteller who can tell a predictable tale with tension and humor. Glass's illustrations are lavish and worth a study.

Europe

Perhaps the most well known of the European tricksters is a cunning fox, known as Reynard. He was immensely popular as a literary figure in Northern Europe in the Middle Ages but predates that period as a character. Reynard was believed to be up to his mischief during Roman times! William Caxton is credited with making the first translation into English of tales about Reynard in 1481. Given that these tales are still being printed today it is safe to say that Reynard holds his own in the world of the crafty.

Picture Books: Europe

Hastings, Selina. (1990). *Reynard the Fox*. Illustrated by Graham Percy. New York: Tambourine Books. Reynard the Fox cast a long shadow over the land. "It was a shadow that moved fast and dangerously. No one in the animal kingdom had escaped without some injury to himself, to his family, or friends." Now the animals were both angry and frightened, so they petitioned the king to bring this slippery subject to justice. The royal Lion was willing to try sending out Bruin the Bear, Tibert the Cat, and the fox's nephew Grimbard, the badger. Bruin and Tibert's efforts were subverted because Reynard tricked them by appealing to their natures. Grimbard succeeded only in bringing in the fox so he could trick the king! Reynard lived to try his tricks again. This lengthy text is accompanied by stylish illustrations.

Cambodia

Cambodia is a country with a long history of being subjugated by strong neighbors and its own rulers. The most recent example of the latter was the savage rule of the Khmer Rouge from 1975 to 1979, a rule in which many thousands of Cambodians died. A theme that recurs and recurs in the stories of these people over time is that of the small, nimble person or animal who is able to outdo the stronger opponent by virtue of a quick wit.

Picture Books: Cambodia

Ho, Minfong & Saphan Ros. (1997). *Brother Rabbit*. Illustrated by Jennifer Hewitson. New York: Lothrop, Lee & Shepard Books. When Brother Rabbit saw the patch of tender rice saplings growing across the river, he had to find a way to get to them. And he did. Crocodile was "called" upon to help and too late did he realize he had been duped. So was the unsuspecting woman who gave all her bananas to the hungry rabbit. And so it went. Rabbit had a glorious day and managed to get home tired but happy and full to tell his tales. Hewitson's illustrations are remarkable for their sense of movement.

Native American

Like other cultures Native American's have their tricksters in folklore and they are numerous. The following are featured in picture book format: Raven, Coyote, Iktomi, and Hare.

Raven

Many cultures consider the raven in a pejorative and distasteful sense because of its association with death and foreboding. Amerinds are an exception. Raven is foremost a shape shifting trickster, but he also serves as a messenger of the Great Spirit.

Picture Books: Raven

McDermott, Gerald. (1994). *Raven*. Illustrated by the author. New York: Scholastic Inc. Raven is revered because he brought light and warmth to the people at a time when all was dark and cold. He invokes his ability to shape change, turning from that of the bird to a pine needle, and is taken in with a drink by the daughter of the Sky Chief. In time he is born as a baby, a grandchild to the mighty Sky Chief. He could deny him nothing including the box in which the light was kept. Seizing his chance, Raven changes back to his true form and flings the sun far into the sky. McDermott has included questions in the text to allow for audience participation as is customary in Native American trickster tales.

Shetterly, Susan Hand. (1991). *Raven's Light*. Illustrated by Robert Shetterly. New York: Athenuem. In this particular retelling Raven forms the earth and the men and animals upon it. He is pleased with his work but saddened by the pervasive darkness. He procures light from the Kingdom of the Day by a deceit. He changes himself into a baby, is born to White Feather, the Great Chief's daughter, and steals the coveted item. But Raven has difficulty convincing the people of the worth of the gift he has brought them. Only a small girl takes up his offer and it is through her vision that the world became a colorful and sunny place.

Coyote

Of all the different tricksters it is Coyote of the Western United States who is the most distinctly American. In real life the animal is a wily, complex creature. He can camouflage himself and can throw his voice so his yelping will not reveal his location. His traditional ties with the people were intimate. So the trickster often referred to as Old Man Coyote is also wily and complex. Some things in the world are explained in terms of his actions—the placement of the stars and the making of mankind to name two. As a shape shifter Coyote can appear both as himself and as almost anything else he wishes. In the stories below he is generally depicted as an animal.

There tend to be more books available that picture Coyote as mischievous and the victim of his escapades than show him to be a positive contributor to the welfare of the world. Most stories featuring Coyote as a creator are discussed in Chapter 6, *The Heavens*. Omitted from the picture book offerings is the highly scatological humor with references to defecation and urination that would have characterized oral retellings of the past.

Picture Books: Coyote

Begay, Shonto. (1992). *Ma'ii and Cousin Horned Toad*. Illustrated by the author. New York: Scholastic Inc. This traditional Navajo story is the tale of a battle between the trickster Coyote, here named Ma'ii, and his cousin, the Horned Toad, who lives on the other side of the mountain. Frustrated because Ma'ii is eating all the corn he has labored long and hard to bring to maturity, Horned Toad tricks the animal into leaving him in peace. He does this by pretending to be happy in Coyote's stomach, all the while torturing and frightening his host. So "even to this day, Ma'ii leaves his cousin Horned Toad alone."

Carey, Valerie Scho. (1990). *Quail Song*. Illustrated by Ivan Barnett. New York: G. P. Putnam's Sons. The plaintive call, "Ki-ruu, Ki-ruu," Quail let out when she cut her foot harvesting grass seed for the winter so entranced passing Coyote he insisted the bird teach it to him. Quail's protests that she was not singing were met by threats and anger three times. "Now teach me your song or I shall swallow you up." Frustrated because she could get no work done, Quail tricked Coyote leaving the animal humiliated and toothless. A twist at the end of the tale completes the sense that justice has been fully served

London, Jonathan. (1993). *Fire Race*. Illustrated by Sylvia Long. San Francisco: Chronicle Books. Some stories attribute the gift of fire to Coyote. "Long ago the animal people had no fire. Day and night they huddled in the dark and ate their food uncooked." Only the Yellow Jacket sisters high atop a snowy mountain had fire and they guarded it jealously. When cunning Coyote spirits a burning piece of oak away they "were screaming mad." But the resolve of the animals and Coyote was too strong for the bad tempered sisters; Eagle, Bear, Mountain Lion, Fox, Worm, Turtle, and Frog outran and outwitted them. And that is why to this day the animal people have a fire around which to tell stories of old.

Sage, James. (1994). *Coyote Makes Man*. Illustrated by Britta Teckentrup. New York: Simon & Schuster Books for Young Readers. In this ancient story it was Coyote who put the final touches on the earth. He scooped out lakes, heaped mountains, and made the grass grow on the tree-covered hills. When complete he asked the animals to help him make his final creation—man.

"What should he look like?" Each animal suggested man should bear his likeness. They could not agree. Finally Coyote shaped an image of man he thought appropriate, out of clay. He gave the creature all the attributes the animals mentioned, plus a brain for wisdom, and the precious gift of life. The animals thought him perfect. In a delicious twist, it is Coyote alone who is not sure about his handiwork!

Stevens, Janet. (1993). *Coyote Steals the Blanket*. Illustrated by the author. New York: Holiday House, Inc. Arrogance is Coyote's undoing in this tale. Coyote experiences a comeuppance when he ignores Hummingbird's warning not to take the beautiful blankets that are lying on the desert rocks ahead. Fancying himself as something of a king, the trickster drapes one of them cloak-like about himself. Angered at losing his cover the rock thunders, "RUMBLE, RUMBLE, RUMBLE," after the thief and a humorous chase ensues. It is only the good graces of Hummingbird that enable Coyote to escape the fury of the rock and to regain his fluffy tail!

Stevens, Janet. (1996). *Old Bag of Bones*. Illustrated by the author. New York: Holiday House, Inc. Even as an old being, Coyote is irrepressible and true to his nature. Feeling his age, "I'm nothing but a bag of bones," Coyote moans. But the sight of the screeching buzzard nearby is enough to bring life to the woebegone creature. He appeals to Buffalo who agrees to give him some strength and youth but no power. This Buffalo does by turning Coyote into one of his own. Quite forgetting his limitations Coyote in buffalo form cannot help showing off and scorning those who claim that age has its compensations. He finds himself back to being an "Old Bag of Bones." Desperately trying to console himself he wanders off to find his grandchildren and then . . . the story is not yet over. Coyote cannot be denied.

Hare

Like Coyote, Hare is the center of traditional trickster cycles but the tales have not been translated into picture book format in the same manner as stories about the "Old Man." One exception is Susan Hand Shetterly's charming tale called *Muwain and the Magic Hare.*

Picture Books: Hare

Shetterly, Susan Hand. (1993). *Muwain and the Magic Hare*. Illustrated by Robert Shetterly. New York: Atheneum. Mahtoqueh (MAH-t'-gwass), the Great Magic Snowshoe Hare of the Woods, plays a game with Muwin the bear. Three times he playfully fools the huge, plump beast, who thinks he may eat one more time, before he begins his hibernation. The fourth time Mahtoqueh appears to Muwain as a Passamaquoddy, this time in the form of a little boy. In his canoe he gently takes the now sleepy, weary bear back to his winter den with its dry leaves and comfortable warmth. The Shetterlys have combined wondrous whimsical art with both the main story and the traditional tales that are skillfully woven into it.

Iktomi

Iktomi, which means spider, is generally depicted as wearing brown deer-skin leggings that are adorned with long soft fringes on each side, a deerskin jacket embroidered with bright beads, and decorated moccasins. He elaborates on this smart appearance by painting his face red and yellow and drawing black rings under his eyes. His long black hair, parted in the middle, is wrapped with red bands and the braids hang over his shoulders.

Iktomi is closely associated with tales from the Plains Indians—the Sioux, Pawnee, Dakota, Cheyenne, and others. The trickster is described by these people as having unusual magical powers, such as the ability to take on any shape. In addition he tends to be characterized as stupid, a vain liar, and clever and noble. The conflicting characteristics exhibited by Iktomi seemed to the Cheyennes to describe the white man. They use the word "veho" to mean both their spider trickster and the white man.

Paul Goble, who has retold many Iktomi, tales has attempted to recreate the Indian storytelling atmosphere and experience in his stories about Iktomi, the trickster. They always begin in a traditional fashion, "Iktomi was walking along." Goble then tells the tale, which is more like a slice of life than a rounded story with a problem and a solution, in large text. He also uses gray italicized print which is placed around the main text for questions and comments the reader is to ask. These questions and comments are designed to encourage audience participation, very much a part of the Indian storytelling experience. Alongside the illustrations of Iktomi and printed in small type are the thoughts that are coursing through his active brain. Mostly these are completely egocentric in keeping with the self-centered nature of this character.

The stories are meant, in the fashion of the Native American, to be tales with a message but they are not to be used as vehicles for moralizing. We can laugh at Iktomi, come to learn his shortcomings, and delight in his single minded pursuit of satisfying himself, but we should not use the stories to preach.

Picture Books: Iktomi

Goble, Paul. (1994). *Iktomi and the Buzzard*. Illustrated by the author. New York: Orchard Books. When Iktomi was heading to a powwow, he was wearing feathers for his Eagle Dance. "People like to see me Eagle Dancing," he was boasting to himself. Such self congratulation was cut short when he reached a river too wide to cross. The trickster did not want to get his feathers wet so he inveigled a buzzard into carrying him across. But his base nature took over during the journey. While they were flying he made fun of the bird's bald head. Mistake. The bird dropped him neatly into a hollow tree and left him there. Never at a loss for long, Iktomi managed to escape after tricking two girls, and the reader is left wondering what he is about to do next!

Goble, Paul. (1991). *Iktomi and the Skull*. Illustrated by the author. New York: Orchard Books. Dressed in his finery Iktomi went off to show himself to the girls in the next village. But his scared horse bolted leaving the trickster stranded away from any camp. Iktomi's loneliness suddenly was forgotten upon hearing a mysterious noise. Inside a nearby buffalo skull the Mouse People were having a pow wow. Their magic stirred Iktomi, and he insisted on joining them by putting his head in the skull and fell asleep! Then, alas, he could not get his head out of the wretched skull! It took a trip down the river and a tongue lashing from his wife before Iktomi was free.

Goble, Paul. (1989). *Iktomi and the Berries*. Illustrated by the author. New York: Orchard Books. Iktomi has delusions of grandeur as he sets out to hunt in the traditional fashion. But all that happens is that the trickster man gets hot and falls into a river. Poor Iktomi. Dripping wet Iktomi sits on the bank where he spies some berries in the water. He finds it difficult to retrieve them, though, even after repeated dives—even all the way to the bottom! When exhausted, Iktomi gives up he looks above him and sees the tree heavily laden with the fruit. Angry beyond measure "how did you get up there," he beats the branches until all the berries fall off, making a lovely feast for the waiting ducks! Poor, poor Iktomi.

Goble, Paul. (1988). *Iktomi and the Boulder*. Illustrated by the author. New York: Orchard Books. This particular story is also a pourquoi tale, an explanation of why bats have faces that are flat and why rocks are scattered all over the Great Plains. Iktomi got hot en route to visiting his relatives. He gave his blanket to a boulder with an explanation that it would keep the huge rock from getting sunburnt. But when it looked like rain Iktomi went back and picked up the article. The angry boulder took off after the trickster man and pinned his legs to the ground. It took some subterfuge and ingenuity on Iktomi's part and a lot of help from bats to set him free. The chasing boulder is quite a common twist in Indian folk tales.

African American

The trickster character most closely associated with the African American folk traditions is Brer Rabbit. It is believed that the character is based on the Great Rabbit or Great Hare, the trickster-hero who plays a pivotal role in the traditional lore of the Native Americans—Passamaquoddy, Lakota, Iroquois, and many others. Little and sassy with only his wit to protect him in Hominy Grove, Brer Rabbit outdid many a foe, Brer Fox and Brer Wolf in particular. Joel Chandler Harris recorded the escapades of the wily rabbit in the late 1800s around a character he created named Uncle Remus. He preserved the Gullah dialect of the nineteenth century storytellers in his tellings. The adventures of Brer Rabbit and his neighbors have been repeated by modern bards with the same zest as exhibited by Harris, but have also brought the language more closely into mainstream English so as to make the tales more accessible to the current reader.

Picture Books: African American

Faulkner, William, J. (1995). *Brer Tiger and the Big Wind*. Illustrated by Roberta Wilson. New York: Morrow Junior Books. The year that no rain came was a terrible time for all the animals—Brer Rabbit, Brer Bear, Brer Racoon, and all kinds of birds. "All the creeks and ditches and springs dried up." Only Clayton Field had "plenty of food and a spring that never ran dry." It was guarded by a large Bengal tiger who menaced everyone who came near him. The tiger was no match, though, for lively Brer Rabbit who was outraged by the injustice of the situation. With wit to spare he outdid the snarling creature, secured some sustenance for the animals, and taught the tiger a lesson about sharing. Wilson has depicted the animal characters as lively and human like.

Harris, Joel Chandler. (1986). *Jump! The Adventures of Brer Rabbit*. Adapted by Van Dyke Parks and Malcolm Jones. Illustrated Barry Moser. San Diego: Harcourt Brace Jovanovich, Publishers. These stories are set "way back yonder when the moon was lots bigger than he is now, when the nights were long and the days were short." Back in those days Brer Rabbit could outdo all other creatures. In this collection of five stories the trickster outdoes Brer Wolf, deceives Brer Fox, and meets his match in Brer Terapin. The illustrations add considerably to this collection. Moser has depicted Brer Rabbit as quite suave; frequently he is dressed up in Sunday clothes and more often than not he is smoking a pipe! All the characters have endearing characteristics and are portrayed in ovals as in an old fashioned photograph.

Jacquith Priscilla. (1981). *Bo Rabbit Smart for True*. Illustrated by Ed Young. New York: Philomel Books. *Bo Rabbit Smart for True* is a collection of stories told by the Gullah featuring the African trickster, Bo Rabbit. An author's note explains that the Gullah people are descendants of the slaves brought to the sea coasts of Georgia and South Carolina. Their lilting speech is distinctive, thought to be a mixture of African and English words and for the uninitiated very difficult to learn. But the character the unique vocabulary gives and the cadence of the language adds much to the telling of the adventures of the tiny trickster. Jaquith has endeavored to keep both but also to keep the stories comprehensible for the average reader. She has succeeded admirably.

Root, Phyllis. (1996). *Aunt Nancy and Old Man Trouble*. Illustrated by David Parkins. Cambridge, MA: Candlewick Press. Root redresses the lack of female trickster characters in her Appalachian tale. Aunt Nancy is the American equivalent of Anansi the spider. She is a wily old woman and a fair match for Old Man Trouble who comes knocking on her door one morning. Everything she does backfires, courtesy of her unwanted visitor. She gets a face full of ashes from the fire, the glass of water falls out of her hand, and the chair breaks beneath her. Undaunted Aunt Nancy finds a reason to be pleased for each turn of events. Then in a coup de grace, she tricks the villain into starting the spring bubbling again. Eventually Old Man Trouble wearies of Aunt

Nancy's relentless good humor and departs thinking he has gained the upper hand. Aunt Nancy merely sits and rocks for a spell.

Stevens, Janet. (1995). *Tops and Bottoms*. Illustrated by the author. San Diego: Harcourt Brace & Company. *Tops and Bottoms* is a wonderfully amusing iteration of the crop division tale described above. Stevens is a lively storyteller and she provides the reader with interesting full-page illustrations.

Holland

Tyl Uilenspiegel is a trickster somewhat of the Robin Hood tradition in that he steals from the wealthy. But unlike Robin Hood he is not generous as he tends to keep his gains for himself. The character is something of a legend in his own country, as his daring and cunning are much admired. The stories about him generally center around the time the Netherlands was engaged in a long and tedious war for independence from Spain. Many towns and villagers were under siege by the Spanish army. Tyl Uilenspiegel tended to trick them in some fashion out of their advantage. For example, in one Christmas tale the rascal filled the Spaniards' cannons with food and then goaded the soldiers into firing them. Soon the villagers who were held hostage by their enemy and were starving, were surrounded by all kinds of delectable food stuffs courtesy of their foes!

Picture Books: Holland

Williams, Jay. (1978). *The Wicked Tricks of Tyl Uilenspiegel*. Illustrated by Friso Henstra. New York: Four Winds Press. Williams has told four stories about the "wicked" Tyl Uilenspiegel whose name means "Owl's Mirror" or the moon. Tyl's typical and cheerful mode of operation is to do something outrageous which incurs the wrath of those he has tricked. Thwarted in their original purpose, they demand some recourse which the trickster provides in abundance. For instance, Tyl explained to the villagers he would walk a 30 foot rope blindfolded and then he proceeded to walk it as it was placed along the ground. Angry villagers of Edam where the deceit had been perpetrated demanded more. This Tyl delivered grandly by tricking the Spanish soldiers, who were holding a nearby castle, by creating so much confusion that the villagers were able to overpower their enemy!

Jamaica

Anansi, the Spider, so well known in Africa is also a trickster in Jamaica and is just as feisty in that small land as he is on the large continent.

Picture Books: Jamaica

Makhanlall, David, P. (1988). *Brer Anansi and the Boat Race*. Illustrated by Arnelia Rogato. New York: Blackie and Son, Ltd. Brer Anansi finds the flood that chases all the animals from their homes to be an opportunity for self-improvement. He challenges Brer Rabbit and Brer Bear to a boat race. As the friends are weighed down with their supplies, Anansi suggests they store them on a table in the river until after the competition. When the rabbit and the bear strain away, they realize that their adversary is not with them. When they return to collect their belongings, they find that they are missing! Anansi, of course, is a picture of innocence but the pair know they have been duped.

Japan

One of the trickster characters of *Old Japan* is reputed to have been a real person, a judge called His Honorable Honor Ooka Tadasuke. His methods of dispatching justice were as unusual and as imaginative as the crimes on which he was asked to pass judgement. Invariably he tricked the criminal into confessing before the rogue had time to think upon what he was doing.

Picture Books: Japan

Edmonds, I.G. (1994). *Ooka the Wise*. Illustrated by Sanae Yamazaki. New Haven: Linnet Books. The stories I. G. Edmonds has relayed in this readable text all focus on the judge, Ooka, who is able to achieve much—from outwitting an owner of a tempura shop who wants to charge a student for stealing a smell, to tricking a thief into revealing that he was at the scene of the crime when he said he was not. Ooka is a particularly endearing character in that he takes the side of children and the poor and the oppressed. He is extraordinarily fond of his grandson and has a hand in helping the boy grow into a fine man, a person without pomp or malice.

Malaysia

The tiny mouse deer, the hero-trickster of the tale by Day reviewed below, is found throughout South East Asia and is held in great affection.

Picture Books: Malaysia

Day, Noreha Yussof. (1996). *Kancil and the Crocodiles*. Illustrated by Britta Teckentrup. New York: Simon & Schuster Books for Young Readers. Kancil, the mouse deer is best friends with tortoise, Kura-Kura, and the two find themselves desiring some juicy fruit on a hot day. Unfortunately for the pair the rambutan tree bearing the said fruit is across the river occupied by a bevy of crocodiles. Kancil tricks the crocodiles into forming a bridge with their bodies and the two animals walk sedately across to the far bank. In a delicious twist the pair remember when they are heading toward the fruit that they have no way of getting back to the other side!

Peru

In Peru the traditional animal trickster is sometimes considered to be a mouse, sometimes a rabbit, and sometimes a guinea pig. Rebecca Hickox, in her story called *Zorro and Quwi*, has made the guinea pig the hero.

Picture Books: Peru

Hickox, Rebecca. (1997). *Zorro and Quwi*. Illustrated by Kim Howard. New York: Doubleday Book for Young Readers. When Quwi, the guinea pig, was caught in the farmer's garden and set in a trap, Zorro was ecstatic. Finally, the fox could get his hands on the beast he had been seeking for many nights. But Zorro did not account for Quwi's quick wit. The guinea pig explained he was waiting to marry the farmer's daughter but was an unwilling party to the arrangement. Zorro quickly agreed to take Quwi's place thinking of an easy life in the house. It was not to be, of course! Three more times, and humorous times at that, the little guinea pig was able to trick the hapless fox until finally Zorro decided that Quwi would be too tough as a meal anyway.

The Young Boy as Trickster

The young boy or lad goes by many names and is a familiar presence in folk tales. This character is often depicted as the youngest of three brothers and sometimes as a prince. He is frequently regarded as lazy and/or stupid, but also sometimes as a person of considerable imagination who gains advantage in altercations through wit rather than energy. In short, the boy is something of a trickster. Opponents in the various adventures experienced by the young boy are often giants, typically large, greedy, and stupid, who were very much alive in the imagination of the peasant of centuries past.

Jack or his cultural counterpart is constantly growing young. He sometimes catches a wife and sometimes he does not. Irrespective of his marital success he was, and is, always looking for adventure.

Figure 1: The Young Boy

Country	Name of Young Boy
America	Jack or John
Canada	Ti-Jean
England	Jack
France	Louis
Germany	Hans
Latin America	Pedro or Juan
Norway	Askelad or Askeleden translated as Boots in English
Russia	Ivan
Spain	Juan

English Jack

Jack first appears in rhyme in fifteenth century England in a book called "Jack and his Step-Dame." Jack, killing giants, was regular fare in the cheap chapbooks that were intended for the lower classes and hawked by peddlers and itinerant merchants in eighteenth century England. In addition make believe letters attributed to Jack appeared in 1744 in *A Little Pretty Pocket Book*, the first book published specifically for children by John Newbery. From this beginning, Jack's escapades became the signature stories of the English story book tradition. Jack was then and remains now a timeless figure.

Picture Books: English Jack

Galdone, Paul. (1974). *The History of Mother Twaddle and the Marvelous Achievements of her Son Jack*. Illustrated by the author. New York: Houghton Mifflin. Galdone has told a version of the traditional *Jack in the Beanstalk* in amusing verse. Old Mother Twaddle, Jack's mother, finds a sixpence and bids Jack to go and buy a goose. Once he has gone to the fair "She hastened with onions / And sage to prepare / A savory stuffing / For the delicate treat / And thought of what glee / Of the tidbits she's eat." Jack, of course, confounds her expectations, at least initially. After he had climbed the beanstalk, the young lad cuts off the head of the giant and marries the maiden who had helped him. In between Jack was able to invite his mother up the beanstalk "With a promise of goose / And a bottle of wine." All ends well!

Kellogg, Steven. (1991). *Jack and the Beanstalk*. Illustrated by the author. New York: Morrow Junior Books. An author's note explains that this version of *Jack and the Beanstalk* is based on the classic from a collection edited by Joseph Jacobs. This recent retelling has maintained the language of the older time period and the whimsical character of the tale is intact. Kellogg's illustrations are yeasty and dramatic; the ogre is truly grotesque, his wife haughty, and Jack's mother homely. The author/illustrator has added a cheeky twist at the end that will evoke a smile from the reader. "The ogre fell down and broke his crown and the beanstalk came tumbling after." In this version Jack is able to marry a princess because of his new found wealth.

Schenk de Regniers, Beatrice. (1987). *Jack the Giant Killer*. Illustrated by Anne Wilsdorf. New York: Atheneum. Beatrice Schenk de Regniers has included some amusing information about giants in her retelling of one of the most famous of the Jack stories, *Jack the Giant Killer*. Each day when the sun goes down a giant from the island comes to steal corn, hogs, sheep, and dogs from the people of Cornwall. Even the odd child has been eaten whole. Only young and adventurous Jack dares to challenge the monster. He teases and entices Giant into a big pit covered with a heap of sticks and straw. When his foe is helpless at the bottom Jack "raps the Giant on the head. The wicked Giant is very dead" and Jack, of course, is a hero.

Schenk de Regniers, Beatrice. (1985). *Jack and the Beanstalk*. Illustrated by Anne Wilsdorf. New York: Atheneum. The spirit of the boy called Jack is fully revealed in the opening verse, "Here's a story about / A boy named Jack, / Bold as brass, / Sharp as a tack." This iteration of the story of a cheeky lad who outwits a giant and has gold aplenty for the rest of his days is told in engaging verse. It is a rather long text but the conversational style makes the reader feel invited to the happenings. In this version the giant falls down dead, "an ugly sight." Schenk de Regniers remains true to the folk tale tradition of swift and terrible retribution of the foolish and the unjust. Overall this is a satisfying book.

Wells, Rosemary. (1997). *Jack and the Beanstalk*. Illustrated by Norman Messenger. Great Britain: DK Publishing, Inc. In this particular iteration of the most well known of all of Jack's adventures, the hero and his mother are left destitute when the giant, who lives in the sky, reached down and plucked up Jack's father. When Jack climbed the remarkable beanstalk to the giant's castle, he heard a sad singing and the sound of a harp. Jack's mother assured him that was his father making music; Jack had a profound reason to return to the castle. Indeed, Jack's father was most pleased to be rescued although the pair barely escaped the ogre's wrath intact. But in the way of *Jack and the Beanstalk* stories, when Jack chopped the beanstalk down, the "giant toppled into the hills and was never heard from again." Messenger's illustrations add much to this telling.

American or Appalachian Jack

The American Jack made the trip with English settlers and is frequently found experiencing his adventures in the southern mountains of Appalachia. Both he and the people of the mountains are colorful and for this reason some background is both interesting and necessary to fully appreciate the Jack stories.

Jack tales were typically passed on orally and are as varied as the storytellers who made them come alive. Storytelling served at least two purposes in pioneering mountain life. When the tales were told in the evening after the day's work was completed they served as entertainment. But the telling of tales was also a vehicle to ensure work was done. Spirited Jack would keep children amused and on the job while they helped with communal tasks such as stringing beans for canning or threading them to make "leather britches" or dried pods.

Appalachian Mountain tales can be truly appreciated only when they are told orally by mountain folk who speak in their patchwork English. In their unique dialect, tellers talk about "bresh" for undergrowth, a mantle piece as a "fireboard," a "painter" as being a mountain lion, an old fashioned bucket as a "piggin," and baking soda as "sody sallyratus." In an attempt both to duplicate the feeling engendered by a live storyteller and to capture the flavor of the region, the retellers of Appalachian Jack tales often include these typical local phrases and sayings. The challenge for the reteller is formidable—how to preserve the character and essence of the story while making it accessible to an audience outside of the region. Gail Haley has an entertaining introduction to the mountain dialect at the end of her collection called *Mountain Jack Tales*.

Picture Books: Appalachian Jack

Compton, Joanne. (1995). *Sody Sallyratus*. Illustrated by Kenn Compton. New York: Holiday House. The Comptons have a story of the time Jack's two brothers were sent to buy some *sody sallyratus* or baking soda so their Ma could bake some biscuits for breakfast. "I done run out," hollered their mother. This errand entailed crossing the bridge over Cold Water Creek, under which was hiding "the biggest, ugliest bear" eyes ever laid upon. In glee the furry beast gobbled up the brothers and then Ma when she went looking for her sons. It took nimble Jack only a couple of minutes only to trick that old bear into tumbling over in the creek and letting Tom, Will, and their mother pop out safe and sound. They were delighted until they realized that they still did not yet have the *Sody Sallyratus!*

Compton, Joanne and Kenn. (1993). *Jack the Giant Chaser*. Illustrated by the authors. New York: Holiday House, Inc. In the practice of story-tellers everywhere, the Comptons have taken an old tale and adapted it to local conditions. Their version of *Jack the Giant Chaser* is an iteration of a Grimms' tale and one that is oft told because it is so engaging. In an attempt to draw attention to himself Jack boasted he had "killed me seven with one blow!" He failed to mention "the seven" were only catfish. Impressed with his prowess the townspeople pressed Jack into the task of ridding the area of the mean old giant on Balsam Mountain. "Since everybody thought he was a hero he figured he'd have to try and act like one." And he did. Through wit and nimble thought, Jack frightened away the giant "across the creek, over the ridge, and past the state line." He never did return.

Davis, Donald. (1995). *Jack and the Animals*. Illustrated by Kitty Harvill. Little Rock, AK: August House Little Folk. Grandma, who lives in a big log house in the mountains, is the storyteller of this well known story. Over supper cooked outside she tells her grandchildren about the time Jack goes off to seek his fortune, although unsure what that was. On the way he gathers up a series of animals who each claim age as a problem. The hungry group scares off in humorous fashion a band of robbers encountered in an isolated farm house. The animals can then lay claim to the abode and all the riches inside. Jack's fortune, not to mention the animals freedom, have certainly been won.

Haley, Gail E. (1986). *Jack and the Bean Tree*. Illustrated by the author. New York: Crown Publishers, Inc. The classic *Jack and the Bean Stalk* is called here *Jack and the Bean Tree*. Embellished with colorful language ("We'll ma'am, my name's Jack. I've spent the day climbing my bean tree to get here, and I'm plum wore out."), and lush, detailed illustrations, the tale is an interesting read. Haley has provided a twist in that Jack and his mother are described as being alone because the father and brothers are away at the war. This is a situation that will change at the end of the book as have their fortunes with arrival of the magic beans.

Illustrated Texts: American Jack

Haley, Gail. (1992). *Mountain Jack Tales*. Illustrated by the author. New York: Dutton Children's Books. Haley has relayed a collection of Jack Tales through the mouthpiece of Poppyseed, an old storyteller of the Appalachian Mountains. Poppyseed lives "just off the highway a little piece, up a dirt road, past the granddaddy oak and crooked persimmon tree." Haley is native to the area and has managed through her characters to capture the attitudes, speech, and outlook of the mountains. Some of the Jack tales have a familiar ring; there is an iteration of the flying ship story and one of the battle with the Northwest Wind. Others are less well known. The story called *The Lion and the Unicorn* features characters not often associated with mountain tales.

The African-American Jack

In contrast to his white counterpart the African-American Jack is not fighting giants, dragons, or ogres, but doing battle with a corrupt society. Jack, sometimes known as *High John the Conqueror,* is a trickster of the finest order and a cheerful one at that. High John is a slave on an unnamed planation in the Mississippi Delta who can out do his ol' massa anytime they meet. In the *High John* stories that event is made explicit. For this reason the African-American Jack stories were known generally only to slaves and largely kept under cover.

Besides being a cheerful human being and intelligent opponent *High John* is often described as a *be* man, which is why he commands so much respect. In a collection of African American tales called *High John the Conqueror*, Julius Lester depicts *High John* this way. He would "be here when the hard times come, and be here when the hard times are gone. No matter how much the white folks put on him, John always survived" (p. 93). John did this by working as hard or harder than any man before him at times. But on other occasions he was up to as little slaving as he could. Mysterious fires of barn and house, crops destroyed unaccountably, and disappearing vegetables were common and could be laid at the feet of the trickster. For his part *High John* would deny all knowledge of such doings and no one could ever connect him to them!

Illustrated Text: African American Jack

Sanfield, Steve. (1989). *The Adventures of High John the Conqueror*. Illustrated by John Ward. New York: Orchard Books. Steve Sanfield is one of the few authors to put together stories about this one character. In his telling of 16 short stories *High John* is compromised only once (or at least tells the truth only once), when he tries to declare himself defeated. In this tale, *In A Box*, John's action of being self-effacing wins him a bet and makes the master a rich man. Sanfield has provided the reader with an introduction and background to each story that is of considerable interest. For example, the origin of the term "coon" as referring to slaves is explained in lively fashion. While the expression became derogatory and racially charged, it once was a term, albeit a grudging one, of respect.

Latin American Pedro

The young boy trickster of Latin American stories is *Pedro Urdemales,* which means "weaver of evil" in Spanish. But *Pedro,* like others of his kind, is not so much evil as self-serving. Any plans and schemes he comes up with are directed merely at his survival. And survive handsomely he has. The first recorded mention of *Pedro* comes from Spain of the 1100s, and his adventures have been the grist of storytellers for many years. Like the Appalachian Jack, *Pedro* migrated, traveling with the Spaniards who sailed to the Americas. Unlike Jack, he frequently went by different names or monikers: *Pedro de Malas* (Peter Wickedness) and *Pedro Malasartes* (Peter Evilarts), to name two.

Pedro chose as his prey those who were rich and powerful. In a Latin American setting this meant the greedy land owner who employed the peasant, a foreigner or gringo, the priest, and town officials such as the mayor. Also *Pedro* often chose to trick those people who were riding horses as horses suggested wealth.

Picture Books: Latin Jack

Brusca, María Cristina and Tona Wilson. (1995). *Pedro Fools the Gringo and Other Tales of a Latin American Trickster.* Illustrated by María Cristina Brusca. New York: Henry Holt & Company. Some of the tales in this collection have retained their slightly bawdy elements, a feature which will no doubt appeal to young readers. For example, *Pedro* relieves himself on the side of the road and covers up the deposit with his hat, holding it down with great show. He then convinces two well dressed men riding toward him that he is hiding a golden partridge. He also convinces them to lend him a horse so he can fetch his brother to help him move the golden bird. Off rides *Pedro,* never to be seen again! A feature of this collection is that some of the same characters reappear. The men who were forced by their own curiosity and greed to pick up *Pedro's* waste, come back increasingly angry at each appearance.

Brusca, María Cristina and Tony Wilson. (1992). *The Blacksmith and the Devil.* Illustrated by María Cristina Brusca. New York: Henry Holt and Company. This Latin American story has a central character called Juan, also a name used for the young boy from this part of the world. Juan Probreza is a blacksmith whose life takes a turn when he shoes the mule of San Pedro, guardian of the gates of heaven. Juan Probreza is offered three wishes by the saint who urges him to use one "to go to heaven." Juan refuses. He is then directly offered a bag of gold and twenty years of youth for his soul by the devil. Juan Probreza gleefully accepts. In time he manages to use his three wishes to trick old Satan. But the story is not yet over!

Russian Ivan

Ivan is in every sense of the word the young boy—stupid, lazy, resourceful, and cunning altogether. With his tendency to idleness he likes to spend his time on the warm stove so closely associated with Russian peasant life and storytelling, but he can succeed when he must. He can consort with the Tsar or outwit a foolish wife with love. Thus many epithets are linked to the name: Daft Ivan, Simple Ivan, Ivan the Fool and every so often, Ivan the Innocent or Prince Ivan. Ivan has always been a part of Russian life and significant to the people. The bakhari or storytellers used Ivan as a vehicle to demonstrate that the world order could be turned on its head; with wit and cunning a peasant could become the equal of a ruler when he marries into nobility.

A particularly interesting tale about Ivan which provides a glimpse into his character centers on his ownership of a magic horse, Silver Roan, who could flash fire and smoke from his eyes and nostrils. When the Tsar announced that he would hand his daughter in marriage to anyone who could snatch her veil from a great height, Ivan took up the challenge. He called to Silver Roan and with magic climbed into his ear. He also changed from his typically scruffy and dirty state into a handsome man. With such magical assistance he was able to succeed. Upon winning the contest, Ivan went back to obscurity and his usual untidy condition. To track down the young winner, the Tsar held a lavish banquet which Ivan attended behind the stove in the feasting hall. But Ivan the fool used the veil to wipe his tankard and was identified. He was awarded the prize!

Picture Books: Russian Ivan

Crouch, Marcus. (1989). *Ivan*. Illustrated by Bob Dewar. Oxford, England: Oxford University Press. Every Ivan from the clever prince to the dullard is represented in this immensely readable collection of stories. Crouch has a knack of telling the stories in the way of a teller; his tone is conversational and personal. Some of the tales have a familiar ring. *A Little Vixen* is a variation of the well known *Puss in Boots,* while others enjoy less currency perhaps because they are slightly bawdy. One of the stories, *Three Brides for Three Brothers,* is a robust tale that includes one other famous Russian character, the awful witch, Baba Yaga. The final story is a treasure and provides a satisfying ending to the collection.

Hall, Amanda. (1981). *The Gossipy Wife*. Illustrated by the author. New

York: Bedrick/Blackie. Ivan has a gentle side as portrayed in the amusing and oft told story about his treatment of his foolish wife. Ivan has a problem—his wife cannot keep a secret. When he discovers a chest of gold in the forest, Ivan knows it will be impossible to keep the news from the greedy landlord once Katarina hears of it. So he plays a trick upon his unsuspecting spouse, the net effect of which is to exasperate the landlord and to reduce Katarina's credibility to zero with the villagers. The gold, however, is secure and keeps the pair in comfort for the rest of their days!

Langton, Jane. (1992). *Salt*. Illustrated by Ilse Plume. New York: Hyperion Books for Children. *Salt* revolves around the youngest of three brothers, Ivan, considered a fool in the family because he asks so many questions. "Is the world round or flat? How high is the sky?" The rich merchant father sends the two elder boys off in fine ships with cargo to sell and trade; to Ivan he gives a mean boat and a load of wooden spoons! But it is Ivan who prevails when he discovers an island of salt which he uses to win a princess bride, secure a valuable cargo, and fight off a giant. In addition, Ivan manages to have his burning questions answered!

Ransome, Arthur. (1968). *The Fool of the World and the Flying Ship*. Illustrations by Uri Shulevitz. New York: Farrar, Straus and Giroux. "The Fool of the World" is the youngest of three sons and considered stupid. But, "God loves simple folks," and the boy confounded expectations by procuring the hand of the Czar's daughter who "loved him to distraction." Such good fortune smiles after the fool heeds the advice of the ancient man to whom he is kind on the road. The "Fool of the World" acquires a flying ship, a condition for the hand of the royal bride, lots of interesting and amusing experiences, and the respect of the Czar and the court.

San Souci, Robert, D. (1992). *The Tsar's Promise*. Illustrated by Lauren Mills. New York: Philomel Books. Ivan is featured as a prince in this story, born to the Tsar Kojata, who inadvertently gave the child away to a fierce demon. As a young man Ivan was called upon to break his father's ill considered agreement. This he does in dramatic fashion, but only with the help of a beautiful girl, Maria, who had also been stolen by the same vile demon. Three times the demon asked impossible tasks of the tsarevitch and three times Ivan was able to achieve them with the magic of his lovely friend. The pair finally broke the evil one's power and lived happily ever after. This text is enhanced by glorious, luminous illustrations. Of particular interest are the number of fairy tale creatures that are present in this story besides the demon, trolls, and a chimera, to name two.

Winthrop, Elizabeth. (1997). *The Little Humpbacked Horse*. Illustrated by Alexander Koshkin. New York: Clarion Books. Ivan learned that the little horse he came to own will "be your wisest counselor" and he will "keep you safe and warm for the rest of your days." Indeed it came to pass. Ivan went to work for the Tsar, a greedy man who wanted yet more and more wealth. When the counselors falsely told the Tsar that Ivan had been boasting he could procure some treasures the Tsar pined for, Ivan was sent to procure them. His finest catch was his third, the Tsarevna who rowed a gold boat with silver oars, with whom he fell deeply in love. But, she could not be his. Such was the case until the little horse explained to Ivan how to deal with the situation. Then Ivan and the Tsarevna were married and they lived long and wise lives together.

Scandinavian Boots

Few stories in the picture book format exist about Boots, so called because he frequently wears long ones, but at least two are rousing tales and would appeal to children.

Picture Books: Scandinavian Boots

Conover, Chris. (1984). *The Wizard's Daughter*. Illustrated by the author. Boston: Little, Brown and Company. The cruel wizard of the North stole all there was in the world for himself, and the country folk had not enough to eat. It was up to Boots, the poor son of a farmer, to break the wizard's magic. This he was able to accomplish with the help of the wizard's daughter who lived as a prisoner in a palace in the bottom of the sea and kept her father's magic secrets. *The Wizard's Daughter* has many of the motifs associated with folk lore—shape shifting, the location of a heart outside of the body for safety, the three riddles, and most significant, the happy ending.

Kimmel, Eric, A. (1992). *Boots and His Brothers*. Illustrated by Kimberly Bulcken Root. New York: Holiday House. Three brothers set out to seek their fortune. Two of the siblings, Peter and Paul are rough and rude; one called Boots is not. It is the gentle manner of this third son that wins over an old woman on the road who directs all the brothers to the castle where they could earn their weight in gold. Their task is to cut down a huge tree, dig a well, and fill it with sweet water. Only Boots is successful. He alone earned and took the advice of the elderly sage. Besides wealth he gains the crown of the grateful king "and a very good king he was, too." The brothers became the keeper of the dogs that had chased them away—a fitting end for the uncouth pair!

Texts Cited

Lester, J. (1970). *Black Folktales*. Illustrated by Tom Feelings. New York: Grove Press.

Mollel, T. M. (1998). *Shadow Dance*. Boston: Houghton Mifflin.

5

Tall Tales

Tall tales, which take a happening and stretch it beyond all credible levels, found a natural home in the young and raw United States. Gathered around a campfire individuals of the pioneer west would swap "windies," which could be either a story or just mere observations. Under the convention that governed such tellings, the raconteur had to include himself as being there when the event happened and to tell it with all seriousness. A storyteller was particularly revered if he could maintain his poker-face demeanor when making preposterous claims such as, "I know a woman who is so small she hides in the barrel of her rifle when the sheriff comes looking for her." He was also much honored if he could match tale for tale in a story swap.

History of the American Tall Tale

Tall tales, boastful in nature, are often constructed around actual individuals. The evidence for the activities of the tall tale hero is frequently sketchy, however, and he or she gained wide currency only through concerted efforts of journalists and oral storytellers. This is particularly the case with people whose exploits were celebrated before the Civil War. A number of individuals were so deified; Mike Fink, a keelboatsman of the Ohio and Mississippi rivers during the 1820's is one such character; Davy Crockett, a true ring-tailed roarer, another.

Crockett's rise to the status of wonder person serves as a prime example of legend building and fully demonstrates this phenomenon as it occurred in the United States. Davy Crockett was a salty and admittedly original backwoodsman from Tennessee who was elected to Congress in 1827. He was much celebrated for his courage and ability on the frontier to fight and kill "b'ar." His adeptness in social situations to turn backwood's phrases into colorful and vivid expression was likewise legendary.

There is no doubt of Crockett's ability to do the latter. He wrote in his autobiography (1834) such metaphors as "a new country where every skin hangs by its own tail," or "as little use as pumping for thunder in dry weather." Crockett also was given to wonderfully descriptive hyperbole to make a point— "lean, lank, labber-sided pups, that are so poor they have to prop up against a post and rail fence fore they can raise a bark," or "a chap just about as rough hewn as if he had been cut out of a gum log with a broad ax." In addition, this pioneer character could match stories with the best of tale swappers at a time when such a practice was a highly developed art form.

But there has to be doubt, more's the pity, about Crockett's ability to perform some of the marvelous feats attributed to him. No man has full command over nature and the elements; no one can escape a tornado by riding lightning or drink the Gulf of Mexico dry. Perhaps the most winsome recounting of the woodsman's exploits is the one about how he saved the earth when it froze on its axis. After climbing Daybreak Hill, Crockett squeezed some bear oil on the said axis and returned with a snippet of sunshine in his pocket.

These stories and others like them of the life and times of Davy Crockett, the congressman, frontiersman, and raconteur, became known through many sources. Crockett did publish an autobiography, but subsequent publications (1835 and 1836) about Crockett's life on the plains and the west were fabrication. Likewise the annual almanacs about him that were published until 1856, 19 years after his death were fantasy. The cumulative effect of such a publicity stream was of course to build up a hero that was as large as the big sky under which he lived. Crockett was far from alone in becoming admired by such means.

Picture Books and Illustrated Texts: Davy Crockett

Adler, David A. (1996). *A Picture Book of Davy Crockett*. Illustrated by John and Alexandra Wallner. New York: Holiday House. Adler has provided the young learner with a highly readable account of the life of one of the country's colorful personalities. While he has certainly provided a factual account of Crockett's life, he has done so with zest giving insight into the personality of the man. He has sprinkled the telling with events that give clue to the larger than life character that Davy Crockett was to become. Adler has also provided a succinct account of some of the legends that grew up about the Tennessee woodsman both before and after the storytelling.

Quackenbush, Robert. (1987). *Quit Pulling My Leg!* Illustrated by the author. New York: Prentice-Hall Books for Young Readers. This text is a brief illustrated biography. Davy, always a precocious child and fiercely independent, is described here as being one of a large family. He poked his first bear at the age of three, and told "leg pullers" from the time he could talk. He frequently worked off the debts his father had incurred by undertaking cattle drives and performing farm labor. Crockett's escapades in congress are described in lively fashion as are the personal details of his life. Crockett's death at the Alamo is the closing account in this interesting book.

Function of the Tall Tale

Why is it that such blatant journalistic practices that gave support to characters that were obviously fabricated were not only condoned but flourished? Three reasons can be identified.

- National character building
- Entertainment
- Politics

National Character Building. The tall stories nourished the hunger of a pioneering people to fashion an identity in a new land that was harsh and unforgiving. If people were to survive and flourish in such a place they had to be self-reliant, nationalistic, and physically strong. Crockett and his contemporaries certainly exhibited all of these traits and became symbols for the national character.

Entertainment. In addition to fashioning a national character, the exploits of individuals in tall tales served as fruity entertainment. Newspapers frequently published folk tales and local legends as news items or human interest stories. By way of example, a story entitled "How Sandusky Was Saved From the Famine" appeared in the Norwalk, Ohio, *Experiment*, January 27, 1857. The article described the port of Sandusky as being tried by drought and famine. No ships could enter and there were no land routes available so the place was shut off. The report was as follows:

> Wild hogs from the neighboring woods tantalizingly trotted to the bay for water. All soon became blind from the vast fields of fine sand that lined the bay, save for one dim-sighted leader. A blind hog took the leader's tail in his mouth, another followed suit behind the second, and so on until the whole drove was accounted for. One day while the line of hogs was making its way to the bay, a bold Scintiscan fired at the leader's tail and amputated it close to the body. Rushing forward the man grasped the remnant still hanging from the second hog's mouth, and began gently pulling. The drove of hogs started forward like a train of cars, and the sharpshooter led them back to the famished natives.

The attention to local detail obscures the fact that the story is merely a variant on a much told tale whose origins are European. Still, such journalistic windies had an inescapable charm.

Political Purposes. Tall tales served political and social leaders well. Benjamin Franklin was known to take delight in using them to satirize the ignorance of Englishmen about the New World. In 1765 he wrote "the very tails of the American sheep are so laden with wool, that each has a little car or wagon on four wheels, to support it and keep it off the ground." Franklin also provided an "authentic" description of an amazing leap of a magnificent whale pursuing codfish up Niagara Falls. His parody concluded that this experience was deemed a fine spectacle of nature by those who witnessed the event.

Abraham Lincoln was also a well known proponent of the windie, a reputedly skilled storyteller and a lover of the art form. His vast repertoire, which tended to reflect his prairie roots, were frequently well known stories—tales about men who could outrun rabbits when chased by an irate farmer with a weapon, for instance. The President was also particularly adroit at turning aside an awkward political situation with a story grounded in his modest roots. He reportedly did this when asked about his intentions for Jefferson Davis after the surrender of the Confederacy. Davis' situation put him in mind, he said, of a small boy who caught a coon and hoped it would escape so he would not have to kill it (Dorson, 1971).

So the tall tale is well grounded in the history of the land and is very much part of the American frontier psyche. The stories cannot in the true sense of the word be considered folk tales or the characters folk heroes. For this reason American tall tales are sometimes known as fakelore. They have not been fashioned by time and numerous retellings over the centuries, but their hold on a place in the hearts of contemporary audiences is tenacious.

Significant Tall Tale Characters

There are some notable characters associated with the tall tale. Most of these people were associated with activities that were critical to the development of the new land—taming the wilderness, logging, building railroads.

These characters and the minor or more regional ones noted below typically shared a number of characteristics:

- born oversized
- rapid growth to maturity
- precocious ability in chosen field
- courageous and daring
- innovative

These are factors that are brought out in the many stories listed below.

Figure 1: Tall Tale Characters

Character	Association	Achievements	Real Person
Paul Bunyan	logging	invention of many tools of trade cleared huge tracts of land formed the Grand Canyon formed the St. Lawrence River	No
Pecos Bill	ranching	invention of many tools of trade brought law and order to Texas brought law and order to country	No
Johnny Appleseed	orchards	established many apple orchards fine storyteller	Yes
Mike Fink	river boat commerce	enabled development of commerce fearless and courageous fighter	Yes
John Henry	railroad worker	equaled achievements of a machine	Unknown

Paul Bunyan

It is doubtful that Bunyan (Eastern spelling, Bunyon), the gigantic logger with the blue ox by name of Babe, existed as a real person. His persona was first fanned into life by a journalist, James McGillivray, in 1910 as a feature in the Sunday magazine section of the Detroit *News Tribune*. McGillivray drew on stories of the prowess of the mythical Bunyan heard in storytelling sessions when he was in a lumber camp as a young boy.

Bunyan grew further in stature through the exploits attributed to him in a series of advertising booklets penned by W. B. Laughhead, an advertising agent for a lumber company in Minneapolis. The first of these small booklets about Paul's adventures, which were greeted with wild enthusiasm by a reading public, appeared in 1914, and continued for 30 years. Perhaps inspired by Laughhead's success Paul Bunyan tales also became a staple of newspapers and magazines; and in 1924 and 1925, two Seattle authors published full length books about the man. These materials and many subsequent others firmly established Paul Bunyan as a figure in the American consciousness. Over time the stories moved from being somewhat bawdy tales favoring the language of lumber operations to books written for children.

Legend has it that Paul was born on the coast of Maine. His rapid growth to an enormous size as a child forced his parents to take him to the wilderness to find enough room for him to grow. As a man he is reported to have invented the logging trade and many of the innovations associated with the industry, such as the grinding stone for sharpening axes. His camps were reputed to be wonders; the bunkhouses were so large the loggers had to use parachutes to get out of bed and the top stories had to be hinged to allow the moon to pass at night! Paul's accomplishments were notable and many. Besides clearing huge tracts of land, the giant lumberjack formed the Grand Canyon and started the Mississippi River. The former came about after he dragged his peavy, a spiked pole, behind him when he walked from Fargo to Seattle one day. The latter accomplishment was inadvertent.

Paul Bunyan was ably assisted by an ox as oversized as he was. The beast known as Babe, was blue in color. With Babe's help much was accomplished, trees were cleared quickly and fearful critters such as the Gumberoos that lived in the forest folds were vanquished.

While the evidence that the Bunyan tales are grounded in either reality or folklore is slight, the expansive stories about him have certainly retained a folklore-like quality. He is frequently considered the model or at least the inspiration for the other demigods that were added to the rich frontier pantheon.

Picture Books and Illustrated Texts: Paul Bunyan

Emberley, Barbara. (1963). *The Story of Paul Bunyan*. Illustrations by Ed Emberley. New York: Simon & Schuster. Paul Bunyon was "a man so big, he used to comb his long beard with an old pine tree he yanked right out of the ground." Paul is credited with many wondrous deeds that include creating the Mississippi River, floating Boston from Maine to Massachusetts and with the help of his blue ox, Babe, clearing the land "of the Sagus, the Hodags, the Wampus, and the man-eating jack rabbits." No one knows where Paul and Babe went after they finished their work since they disappeared into the deep woods. Emberley's woodcuts in brown and blue are stark and dramatic and, in keeping with the story, outrageously outsized.

Kellogg, Steven. (1984). *Paul Bunyan*. Illustrated by the author. New York: William Morrow & Company. Kellogg begins his retelling of many of the known escapades with Bunyan's birth as an outsize baby in the state of Maine. His meeting with Babe, the blue ox, the fighting with the underground ogres called Gumberoos, the digging of the Saint Lawrence River, the building of the Grand Canyon, and the realization of getting to California are just some of the adventures described. Kellogg has a vigorous style of writing and illustrating that does justice to the broad character of the story.

Rounds, Glen. (1936/1976). *Ol' Paul the Mighty Logger*. Illustrated by the author. New York: Holiday House. This exploration of the life of the mighty logger was first published in 1936 and reprised in 1976. It has only been enhanced by the years. Eleven stories feature Paul and his activities; the first being an account from the author of the need to put the tales on paper. In true windie fashion the narrator is claiming that he knew and worked with Paul and that many of the stories told about him veered from the truth. He feels it his duty to set the record aright! And so he does in very readable fashion telling about any number of events connected with the logging life.

Rounds, Glen. (1984). *The Morning the Sun Refused to Rise*. Illustrated by the author. New York: Holiday House. In his characteristic droll style Rounds has written an original Paul Bunyan tale. The story centers around the fact that one day the sun did not come up because the earth was frozen on its axis. It was up to the mighty logger to figure out how to thaw it out and to get the earth spinning again. The solutions are typically frontier and outsize! Rounds also offers, via his windie, an explanation as to why the country has a range of mountains on each coast and a mid west in between! Line illustrations accompany the improbable adventures as well as several "maps" and "technical drawings."

Pecos Bill

The infamous cowboy who came to be known as Pecos Bill was given birth by the fertile imagination of journalist Edward O'Reilly. Bill is essentially a manufactured hero but one worthy of the fabrication.

Pecos Bill, as the legend goes, was born about the time Sam Houston discovered Texas. In outline form the story is as follows: He was born one of 16 brothers and sisters. Bill's father, Old Man, was feeling crowded the day they discovered some folks had moved in 50 miles away and he uprooted his family. On the westward journey Bill fell out of the wagon while crossing the Pecos River. No one missed him until it was too late to turn back and by that stage Bill had learned to fend for himself. With the help of a coyote, Bill lived wild and free until he was about 10 years of age and in truth thought of himself as one of the furry animals. A cowboy who was passing one day took the man-child back to camp. In short order Bill was able to ride a horse as well as any other, round up cattle with the best of them, and eat his share of griddle cakes for breakfast.

Bill slowly gained notoriety with his activities. The time he roped a train and dangled it in the air, never having seen one before, causing a stir among the folks on board. His scarf was a rattlesnake he had "tamed."

When Bill set out on his life's work, which he determined was to clean up Texas, he did so in brisk fashion. Soon all the robbers in the state had run away so he headed a gang of cowboys to continue the task of making the country safe. And the adventures continue . . . lion wrestling, great feats with a lasso, bronco riding—nothing was too daring or dangerous. Bill's end was an inglorious one though. He laughed himself to death at a city fella who thought that the dogies in the song, "Git Along Little Dogies" were doggies!

Picture Books and Illustrated Texts: Pecos Bill

Dewey, Ariane. (1983). *Pecos Bill*. Illustrated by the author. New York:

Greenwillow Books. Pecos Bill is credited in this telling with inventing the lasso, taming a mountain lion, settling a gang of outlaws, and setting up a cattle farm. In addition, Pecos Bill is believed to have ridden a tornado that crossed the west. The ride ended when the cowboy slid down a flash of lightning, landed with a crack, and formed, according to the legend, the Grand Canyon. Like the prose the artwork is spare. The characters and scenery are presented in browns, beige, and greens, colors associated with the country of the cowboy.

Felton, Harold. (1949). *Pecos Bill Texas Puncher*. Illustrated by Aldren A. Watson. New York: Alfred A. Knopf. Harold W. Felton's *Pecos Bill, Texas Cowpuncher* is a version about Bill's adventures that is somewhat old, published in 1949, and would likely be unavailable except from a library. The text still reads with a freshness and vitality that would make it a useful addition in a class collection. The stories which by the admission of the author may have been "truthened" up a bit, are detailed and cover the time from his birth through his invention of the art of being a cowboy to his marriage to Slue-Foot Sue. A summary of the true character of Bill ends the assemblage.

Kellogg, Steven. (1986). *Pecos Bill*. Illustrated by the author. New York: William Morrow & Company. "Back in the rugged pioneer days when Pecos Bill was a baby, his kinfolk decided that New England was becoming entirely too crowded, so they piled into wagons and headed west." So begins the saga of a boy who was to become the ultimate cowboy. *Pecos Bill* met all challenges equally, except that posed by his bride, Slue-Foot Sue, who wishes to ride Widow Maker. Kellogg has the newlyweds meeting up unexpectedly with *Pecos Bill's* parents at the end of the tale. They all settled in for a "wingding" of a family reunion and the descendants are still on Bill's ranch!

Johnny Appleseed

Johnny Appleseed gained that sobriquet from his custom of planting apple trees in the frontier forests of Ohio and Indiana. Over the course of his lifetime he continually moved his nurseries west to keep ahead of the frontier.

Appleseed was born John Chapman, September 26, 1774, in Leominster, Massachusetts, to a father who had fought in the Revolutionary War. Mrs. Chapman died when Johnny and his sister, Elizabeth, were young and the pair then lived with their stepmother. She was to add 10 more children to the family. When John was 12 the North West Territory was opened up and soon after he set off to claim the wilderness as his own.

John Chapman was a reasonably large man physically and his strength was prodigious, even into old age. He was known as a friend to animals, Indians, and settler alike. He would help distressed wild life find a new home or protect them in one of his campsites. John could speak some native languages and would mediate when relations between the settlers and the Indians were strained. Since he followed the teachings of Swedish philosopher, Emanuel Swedenborg, Appleseed was also considered religious.

There are some folklorists who dispute the gentle image of Chapman conveyed in the popular literature. His appearance to the families he encountered was indeed odd, but he was not believed to be the antisocial eccentric of modern iterations of his story. He was no self ordered pauper, for instance, owning 22 properties by the end of his life. In addition, he spent much time with his half-sister and her family in Ohio.

Robert Price, a biographer of Chapman, noted that many tales about the man circulated among pioneer folks in Ohio and their essence was "hearty and brawny." Such stories indicate Chapman's tolerance for hardship and privation was undoubtedly high, but the man was not slave to such conditions. For instance, he wore Choctaw moccasins and did not go continually barefoot as popularly supposed.

It appears that Johnny Appleseed was not above telling windies of his own and was as much a storyteller as a subject of tales.

Picture Books and Illustrated Texts: Johnny Appleseed

Glass, Andrew. (1995). *Folks Call Me Appleseed John*. Illustrated by the author. New York: Doubleday Books for Young Readers. Andrew Glass has taken Chapman's role in this story about his half brother. Nathaniel came out to the Pennsylvania wilderness at Johnny's request to help him with his seedling business. The poor lad was unprepared for frontier life or his brother's lifestyle. For his part Johnny was unprepared for the young boy's appetite and was forced to take a wild trip to Fort Pitt to replenish supplies. His adventures on the river were characteristically "tall" as he fought cold, helped a wolf, and avoided a "muley" steer. It turns out that Nathaniel was not short of adventures of his own! A band of Indians saved the boy from exposure and starvation. Glass states evidence exists that Nathaniel lived with his brother on French Creek between 1797 and 1800, and his story is based on events of that period.

Hodges, Margaret. (1997). *The True Tale of Johnny Appleseed*. Illustrated by Kimberly Bulcken Root. New York: Holiday House. Hodges' pedantic text adds to the popular myths in her retelling about the man; that Chapman was continually barefoot and poor. What the text does provide is an insight into the legacy of Appleseed and the motivation he had for undertaking the task of creating apple trees for a nation. The obvious pride the people of the mid west have in their native son is reflected in the final page. "When the apple trees make a cloud of white in the springtime, you may still catch a glimpse of something or someone . . . It may be the spirit of Johnny Appleseed come down from Heaven to tend his trees."

Kellogg, Steven. (1988). *Johnny Appleseed*. Illustrated by the author. New York: Morrow Junior Books. Kellogg has portrayed the adventures of the early orchardist without sentimentality. In combination with the lively illustrations, this text is an enjoyable experience.

Lindbergh, Reeve. (1990). *Johnny Appleseed*. Illustrated by Kathy Jakobsen.

Boston: Little, Brown and Company. Emphasis has been given in this iteration, written in verse, of the spiritual nature of Appleseed as he toured the
west planting apple trees. The poem indicates that Johnny believed his calling to seed the land came from God, and it was this strong conviction that
allowed him to endure poverty and hardship for the benefit of others.
Jakobsen's folk art paintings are brilliantly colored, lively, and detailed, making an imaginative complement to this timeless story.

Mike Fink

Mike Fink was a real person and a man who exemplified his times. He won
fame as a marksman early in his life while fighting the British and the Indians
on the Pennsylvania frontier. Later he became known as a fine keelboatsman
on the Ohio and Mississippi Rivers in the 1820's when such vessels were the
main stay of commerce. Fink was one of the "pantheon of frontier gods" created by the press in the years from 1828 through the Civil War.

Fink also had a reputation as a cruel bully, a braggart, and a boisterous
fighter and many tales were told about the man. Stephen Kellogg has relayed
the more positive aspects of the character in his picture book, *Mike Fink*.

Fink's life and adventures are also bound up with Davy Crockett. He is
reputed to have beaten Davy in a shooting match but was unable to get the
better of the redoubtable, Sally Ann Thunder Ann Whirlwind Crockett, Davy's
wife. Fink's end is reputed to be as wild as his life. Fink and a friend by name
of Carpenter were taking turns at shooting a tin cup off one another's head.
Carpenter had first shot and he grazed Fink's scalp. Fink was so enraged that
he shot his friend through the forehead, an act which earned him a bullet
through the heart from one of Carpenter's supporters!

Picture Books: Mike Fink

Kellogg, Stephen. (1992). *Mike Fink*. Illustrated by the author. New York:
Morrow Junior Books. Kellogg's version of Fink's escapades have him training for the life of a keelboatsman by wrestling bears. He fights rapids, man-
eating crocodiles, and snapping turtles on the turbulent upriver journeys, all
the time being singularly successful in gaining and keeping the red feather
that designated him as a champion.

John Henry

John Henry is the subject of one of the most famous folk ballads in American history, variations of which began appearing about 1900. The story goes
thus: John Henry was a black man of prodigious strength who was working
on the Big Bend Tunnel on the Chesapeake and Ohio Railroad in West Virginia. The workmen were using long handled hammers to pound steel drills
into rock to make holes into which explosives could be placed. One day an
experimental steam drill was brought onto the work site, and it was claimed

that it could do the work of 20 men. John Henry took up the challenge and proved that it was possible to dig faster than a machine. In many iterations of this story John Henry won the race but died at the moment of victory in the arms of his devoted wife, Lucy.

Whether the tale is based on an actual event is disputed. It is of little matter. This story first caught the imagination of the public because it is so dramatic and continues to hold it for the same reason. But this snippet of folk lore also resonated because it symbolized the tenacious human spirit of those who tamed the land. Julius Lester has joined the line of storytellers who warm the story of *John Henry* with a particularly compelling picture book iteration.

Picture Books: John Henry

Lester, Julius. (1994). *John Henry*. Illustrated by Jerry Pinkney. New York: Dial Books. "Like a shooting star *John Henry* comes to this world and like a shooting star he leaves it." The famous story of precocious John Henry growing up, his prodigious strength, and race with the steam engine is told in lilting, colorful language, "The air seemed to be dancing to the rhythm of his hammers." Pinkney's illustrations are glorious, magical, and loving.

Sanfield, Steve. (1986). *A Natural Man*. Illustrated by Peter J. Thornton. Boston: David R. Godine, Publisher. Sanfield's version of the life of John Henry is lengthy and intriguing. It is worked around a recurring theme that the tall tale hero prided himself on being a *Natural Man* who could do anything to which he put his mind. From the time he was born a slave, all 33 pounds of him, until he died as a free man fighting for his honor against the steam train, he outdid everyone else. Why, he picked three bags of cotton to everyone else's one, and he guided a tossing boat up the storm riven Mississippi River when no-one else could! True, Henry was a bit of a braggart. But his "do-say was as big as his say-so," so he was forgiven. The pictures are in black and white and they make you feel as though you can still hear John Henry's hammer's ring!

Minor Male Tall Tale Characters

There are a number of other characters who arose to occupy and entertain the popular imagination, particularly at the turn of the century. Some, like their tall tale forbears were born in the fertile minds of writers and journalists—*Febold Feboldson* is one, *Old Stormalong* another. Other characters were real people, gifted raconteurs who were able to create cycles of stories with themselves as the heroes. *Gib Morgan* is one such individual and *Big Mose* is another storyteller of note. While these latter individuals were able to become legends in their own time, they have not generally held the public fancy; perhaps because the spirit and atmosphere of their oral stories could not be captured on a page. Like the characters that preceded them, each is closely associated with an occupation that was significant to the settling of the vast new America.

Figure 2: Minor Tall Tale Characters

Character	Association	Achievements	Real Person
Febold Feboldson	farming	tamed the elements	No
Old Stormalong	shipping	built the Panama Canal	Unknown
Gib Morgan	oil drilling	raconteur	Yes
Big Mose	fire fighting	first urban folk hero	Yes

The stories of these minor tall tale characters tend to be told as part of collections rather than as individual tales. The collections are reviewed below.

Febold Feboldson

Febold was reputed to have been the first white settler west of the Mississippi, the indomitable son of a Swedish immigrant. He settled in a bleak area famous for its dry weather, dust storms, and grasshoppers. To him was given the task of handling this inhospitable climate which turned the country into a man killing, God-forsaken one. He often did this with such measures as tying tornadoes into knots as they galloped over the plains. Besides wrestling with extraordinary weather patterns Febold also took on Indians, politicians, and disease.

Febold Feboldson, like some of his tall tale forbears was the product of an active imagination or perhaps more correctly collective imaginations. His story is the classic one of the process of legend and hero making. He was invented by a lumber dealer in Nebraska by name of Wayne T. Carroll and was patterned after the outsize Paul Bunyan. Like Bunyan he appeared in company advertising, though as a farmer rather than a lumber man. A series of stories by Carroll appeared in 1923 about this doughty farmer in the *Independent*, a newspaper in Gothenburg, Nebraska, and further yarns appeared in the Gothenburg *Times* from 1928–1933. Some of these stories, and there was one a week, a total of 260 tales over this period, came from readers. Perhaps the individual who gave them the most life though was a lawyer, Paul Beath, who published Febold's antics in a number of pamphlets in 1937. His sources were the thousands of stories he heard swapped while he was a young boy serving as a night clerk in a Gothenburg hotel.

Picture Book: Febold Feboldson

Dewey, Ariane. (1984). *Febold Feboldson*. Illustrated by the author. New York: Greenwillow Books. Dewey's text is one of the few in picture book format to explore Febold Feboldson. In a series of seven short stories she explores Feboldson's handling of different weather patterns. She begins with the famous "big snow" windie that claims the snow drifts were 40 feet high and stopping those wishing to prospect for gold from getting to California. The determined farmer went to Death Valley and returned to the Nebraska plains with a wagon full of golden sand which never loses heat. He sold it to the prospectors and they used it to melt the snow! The lack of rain, too much rain, lack of sun, too much sun, lack of wind, too much wind—all adversities were handled with aplomb by Febold!

Gib Morgan

Gib Morgan was a real person. He was a cable driller in the oil industry, an occupation he took up after the Civil War. Morgan's chief claim to fame was that he was a raconteur of some note. His stories were primarily about himself and his experiences on the oil fields. The tales were humorous, extravagant, inflated, fanciful, and had a ring of authenticity about them.

Gib Morgan has not continued his hold on the collective imagination, perhaps because he was so much a part of his own legend; it was not possible to capture the flavor of his fifty or so windies in print. Gib appears in some collections of stories about tall tale characters, frequently under the name of Kemp Morgan, though his colorful nature tends to be obscured.

Big Mose

Moses Humphrey was a volunteer fireman, known as Big Mose, who became the first urban folk hero. Humphrey was given life as the star of a play as Mose the Bowery B'hoy in 1848. The production was titled *A Glance at New York* and it was a grand hit. Following *A Glance* were other plays and stories about Mose in newspapers and booklets. His stature was enhanced by graphics as his picture began to appear on posters and lithographs.

Red headed *Big Mose* was reputed to be huge. Besides being able to hoist around his particular fire engine—the old gal—Lady Washington Engine No. 40, it was rumored Mose could carry streetcars and swim the Hudson River in two strokes. His rough manners and quaint speech were considered his endearing qualities. Gallus, as used by Big Mose, meant grand and for Big Mose much was gallus—the engine, the day, and the battle of the flames were typically gallus such was his zest for life.

Morgan and Mose are what are sometimes called Münchausen figures. They consistently cast themselves into the role of the conquering hero. As listeners repeated their adventures, elaborated upon them, and even attributing many acts to the characters, the mystique around them grew.

Old Stormalong

Old Alfred Bulltop Stormalong, was a jolly sea dog, the greatest of all Yankee sailors. No one really knows if there was such as person as Stormy, who was famous at the time when the vessels were wooden and their sails flew in the wind.

Everything about Stormy was oversize, his physical stature, appetite, ability to dance, catch whales, and his claims on a pedigree. The sailor asserted he could trace his lineage back to the time of Noah! He would boast that his great-great-grandfather helped build the Ark and keep it afloat at the time of the flood.

Old Stormalong's adventures at sea and in exotic places are legion. Among the most notable of his "achievements" is the building of the Panama Canal. This occurred when the ship Stormy was steering, the *Courser,* was caught in a vicious gale. It was blown off course and across the isthmus of land that was then jungle between the Atlantic and the Pacific Oceans. In the process, the ship dug a deep ditch, now known as the Panama Canal!

The major and minor characters noted above do not nearly exhaust the folk heroes that were so much part of the life of the frontier and beyond into the early part of the twentieth century. They tend to be the ones that appear most frequently in collections of stories about the time in America's history when everything was outsized.

While the tall characters differ in as much as each arose from the specific geography of an area or from lore surrounding an occupation, as individuals they have much in common. All are physically strong and have pluck and humor. These characteristics were highly valued at the time. Many of the other characteristics also valued in these tales, use of brawn over brains, the condoning of violence, the complete domination of the land plus the racial and cultural prejudices expressed, are not well regarded in the current social climate. Contemporary retellings tend not to extoll these characteristics as fully as in the past. Nonetheless, the stories endure because they are vital, the characters are fine in heart and spirit. They capture much of what is best in America.

Illustrated Texts: Tall Tales

Noted below are some recent collections of tall tales featuring many of the major and minor characters discussed. It is interesting to note that some of these texts are illustrated using a medium closely associated with the tall tale, that of wood engravings. Many of the materials, such as the almanacs detailing Davy Crockett's adventures were illustrated using a lithographic process invented in 1791. Furthermore, from the 1830's onwards, cartoon-like figures that humorously exaggerated the known characteristics of the individuals were employed. The woodcuts and the cartoon together created a homespun earthy feel that both supported and was reflective of the characters. This same feel is evident in the "new" texts.

Osborne, Mary Pope. (1991). *American Tall Tales.* Illustrated by Michael McCurdy. New York: Alfred A. Knopf. Mary Pope Osborne's collection is illustrated by McCurdy in the traditional woodcut style. Furthermore, the characters are depicted in the exaggerated cartoon format mentioned above. Stormalong is shown as somewhat awkward and completely dominating of the ship upon which he is sailing. Mose is somewhat frightening in his daunting pose wearing a top hat. Osborne has made a special effort in her retellings to downplay the fast living aspects of the life and times of each character and has highlighted the most positive qualities. She provides notes on each story.

San Souci, Robert D. (1991). *Larger than Life*. Illustrated by Andrew Glass. New York: Doubleday. San Souci has told the better known stories about the better known characters in his text *Larger than Life*. The exception is a character well known in Texas but not known nationally. Strap Buckner is a fighter, one of the greatest heroes of his time. "He was the size of a grizzly bear and as strong as 10 wildcats." Legend has it that he ran out of people to fight and out of desperation took on the devil himself. He was to lose, but he gave the bad one an unaccustomed hard time. The women who featured in the lives of the tall tale characters such as Lucy Henry and Slue-Foot Sue have a place in these tellings.

Walker, Robert Paul. (1993). *Big Men, Big Country*. Illustrated by James Bernardian. San Diego: Harcourt Brace Jovanovich, Publishers. Walker tells nine stories about famous tall tale characters from original sources. He also provides the reader with additional information that was not included in the story. For example, Walker states that the oil man Morgan had not visited many of the places in which the windies were set. The author has also provided an introduction that gives the reader a real sense of how the story spread and grew among common folk.

Female Characters

Traditionally women have been under represented in tall tales with only two being mentioned consistently—Sally Ann Thunder Ann Whirlwind Crockett, the wife of Davy Crockett, and the spouse of Pecos Bill, Slue-Foot Sue. They appear both in their own right in collections of stories and as the wives of the famous characters. Other women of note are Annie Christmas, Bess Call, Sal Fink, and Lucy, wife of the steel-driving Henry. Like the male tall tale heroes the women are adventurous. If married, they typically caught the attention of their husband when they were doing something outrageous.

Identifying larger-than-life females who were carved out of the lore of the land is difficult. The women's place and area of concern in the society birthing the tall tales was one of children, hearth, home, and as a helper to her husband. It was not usual to have a woman acting as a warrior, a hunter, or a trickster. Nonetheless, these figures did exist and materials are now being developed that pay the woman her just due as a trail blazer and leader.

Slue-Foot Sue

Slue-Foot Sue was riding a huge catfish down the Rio Grande when she met her cowboy husband. Pecos Bill was immediately love struck and could deny his bride nothing, including a ride on his famous tetchy horse, Widow Maker. The horse lived up to its name and bucked his mount harder than anyone had been bucked before. Sue flew into the sky, almost hitting the moon, and when she landed her steel-spring bustle bounced her back into the heavens. For all anyone knows Slue-Foot Sue is still bouncing! Slue-Foot Sue is featured in Steven Kellogg's picture book story, reviewed below, about her husband, *Pecos Bill*.

Sally Ann Thunder Ann Whirlwind Crockett

Sally Ann Thunder Ann Whirlwind Crockett is likewise an adventurer who arrived in this world the equal and more of any frontier hero. She could out do any of her nine brothers in whatever activity they chose. At nine, finding her horizons limited, Sally Ann set off to explore the world. Her adventures placed her in the path of Davy Crockett, the famous woodsman, and the two were happily wed. Sally Ann's adventures, however, had only begun.

Annie Christmas

It is not clear if Annie Christmas was black or white since both races claim her. And no wonder since she is larger than life; a kind of female *John Henry* in the grasp she has on the imagination. In a tale by Virginia Hamilton, in a collection of African American folk tales called *Her Stories*, she is described in picturesque language as being "coal black and tree tall." She stood 7 feet barefoot, and she weighed 299 pounds. She would tell you she was "the biggest woman in the State of Loo'siana, the strongest that ever lived in New Orleans-town." Annie was a keelboat operator and knew the Mississippi well, like the back of her hand. She could use this same hand to make a hard fist with which she could beat down any boatman on the river.

Like some of her male counterparts and her female counterparts mentioned above, Annie Christmas is believed to be largely fictional although the character was based on a real person. Originally a famous New Orleans whore, Annie developed out of the pen of Lyle Saxon, a writer from Louisiana.

Picture Books and Collections: Female Tall Tale Characters

Dewey, Ariane. (1988). *The Tea Squall*. Illustrated by the author. New York: Greenwillow Books. Dewey has conjured up the notion that the women of the tall tale past get together on an annual basis and discuss events in their lives. They arrive for the event known as a tea squall in predictable fashion— Sal Fink, Mike Fink's outrageous daughter, races past the steamboat on the back of an alligator, Sally Ann Thunder Ann Whirlwind Crockett leaps across the Ohio River. When six of them get together, they try and out do one another with their outlandish tales. "What a winter we had," said Florinda. "It was so cold that ice cream came out when I milked the cow." Their appetites were as large as their stories. Altogether a good time is had by all and the women look forward to their next tea.

Hamilton, Virginia. (1995). *Her Stories*. Illustrated by Leo & Diane Dillon. New York: The Blue Sky Press. Hamilton includes a story about Annie Christmas in this collection of stories about African-American women. This "tall tale" lady, the storyteller reveals, was not without feminine wiles. One evening she shaved off her mustache, put feathers in her hair, and donned a shiny purple outfit and with some girl friends took a trip down the river. In the course of this journey she met and fell in love with the captain of a boat that had become hung up on a sand bar. He did not reciprocate her affection and Annie was not the same again.

Kellogg, Steven. (1995). *Sally Ann Thunder Ann Whirlwind Crockett*. Illustrated by the author. New York: Morrow Books. Aided and abetted by a proud husband, Sally Ann surpassed her already fierce reputation as a fighter! She engaged in a battle of wits and strength with the ferocious Mike Fink and bested her adversary roundly. Kellogg has drawn this version of the tall tale from various iterations that appear in the *Davy Crockett Almanacs* which were highly popular with nineteenth-century readers. He has complemented his vigorous telling with rip-roaring illustrations.

San Souci, Robert, D. (1993). *Cut From the Same Cloth*. Illustrated by Brian Pinkney. New York: Philomel Books. Robert D. San Souci succeeded, after much research, in putting together a fine collection of stories from all ethnic groups in American society that features only women. He calls his text *Cut From the Same Cloth*. His book is divided by region, Northeast, South, Midwest, etc., five districts in all. Three stories under each section are presented; tales of less well known women, characters who are as colorful as their better recognized cousins. Most of these women are physically strong but not outsized in appearance. While some fight, Bess Call and Annie Christmas are predisposed to fisticuffs, most do not. Their strength comes from character, tenacity in the face of hardship, and an indomitable and cheerful spirit. Sweet Betsy from Pike who was ablaze with gold fever endured all manner of difficulties to cross the country to get to California. Pinkney's scratch illustrations provide the text with a homespun feel.

Recent American Windies

Pleasingly for the current generation there continues to be stories published in the American tall tale tradition. These stories glorify the positive characteristics of the genre—humor, free and willing spirits, and the ability to laugh at oneself while down playing the need to achieve outsize physical accomplishments. Some of these new and original tall tales feature women as a way of redressing the lack of stories honoring the contribution of the fairer sex to frontier life.

Picture Books: Recent Windies

Birchman, David F. (1996). *Jigsaw Jackson*. Illustrated by Daniel San Souci.

New York: Lothrop, Lee & Shepard Books. Birchman has a knack for seeing things at a different angle from everyone else. The hero of *Jigsaw Jackson* is a potato farmer from Maine who finds the winters slow. He kept busy playing checkers with the plough horse, listening to opera with the mynah bird, and mending everything in sight—but there still was not much to do. The day that Sean McShaker, jigsaw puzzle salesman, came to town things changed. When Sean found the farmer a whizz at putting jigsaw puzzles together he took him on the road. For a while J. Jupiter Jackson enjoyed it—but he did miss his animals. The ending is both predictable and surprising.

Birchman, David F. (1995). *The Raggly Scraggly No-Soap No-Scrub Girl*. Illustrated by Guy Porfirio. New York: Lothrop, Lee & Shepard Books. The story recalls the days in the early part of the century when folks took a bath once a week in a tin tub on Saturday night. The four children of the farm reveled in the experience after days of playing in the dust. One Saturday night as the family was sitting down for corn bread, chicken 'n dumplings, and blackberry cobbler a knock called them to attention. There stood the filthiest girl anyone had ever seen. She announced herself as *The Raggly Scraggly No-Soap No-Scrub Girl*. She then demolished a huge meal, in company with her raven, danced, and fell dead asleep. But when Mother proposed that she needed a bath her eyes popped open and she bolted—this no-soap, no-scrub girl. The family knew she would be back for Mother makes good cobbler!

Cohen, Caron Lee. (1997). *Crookjaw*. Illustrated by Linda Bronson. New York: Henry Holt and Company. This hyperbolic telling of the adventures of a whaler born Ichabod Paddock provides the reader with both examples of interesting language usage and insights into the superstitions of those who led the life. Ichabod Paddock was an awesome force from the time he was born when "he took his pappy's harpoon for a teething ring." He also dove into Nantucket Sound and swam as "slick as an eel in a barrel of jellyfish." But Ichabod Paddock was no match for Crookjaw the whale, or perhaps the witch who traveled inside the huge marine beast. It took the intervention of his sage wife, Smilinda, to rescue the whaler from the charms and wishes of that evil one!

Day, David. (1991). *The Walking Catfish*. Illustrated by Mark Entwisle. New York: Macmillan Publishing Company. When Hank Blizzard and his gang of River Rats engage the Road Dog gang in a "Big Three Day Lie-Off" it looks as though the visitors are going to win. However, at the last moment on the second day of the competition the scruffy orphan, Hank, tells a preposterous tale about a catfish that can walk. Furthermore, he "produces" evidence that the catfish he showed off was nothing but a baby and that a huge one lives in the river. In the midst of all the tom foolery Hank disappears. The people refuse to have a funeral since they cannot believe that Hank has really been swallowed up by his tale. "Well," says the old man at the end of the story, as he sits and remembers the event. He is obviously perplexed!

Gilchrist, Theo. E. (1978). *Halfway Up the Mountain*. Illustrated by the author. Philadelphia: J. B. Lippincott Company. In a shack halfway up the mountain lived an old man and old woman who were supremely happy together despite the fact that he was slow of movement and she nearly blind. Only one thing made the old man tetchy—his wife cooked beef for dinner each night and he wearied of it. He was to be grateful, however, for the old woman's predilection to sameness one evening when the bandit, Bloodcoe, visited them with meanness in his heart. While the interloper lay sleeping on the stove, the old woman, mistaking him for the daily slab of beef covered him with salt and pepper setting Bloodcoe sneezing. He left the house declaring the devil himself was present, leaving his bag of gold behind.

Issacs, Anne. (1994). *Swamp Angel*. Illustrated by Paul O. Zelinksy. New York: Dutton Children's Books. "On August 1, 1815, when Angelica Longrider took her first gulp of air on this earth, there was nothing about the baby to suggest that she would become the greatest woods woman in Tennessee." Her nickname, *Swamp Angel*, comes from a time when she rescues a wagon train mired in Dejection Swamp. Her lasting fame comes from the fact that she overcame the huge bear, Thundering Tarnation, after a protracted battle, who was terrorizing the settlers. The bear's pelt was too big for Tennessee so *Swamp Angel* moved it to Montana and spread it out in front of her cabin. "Nowadays, folks call it the Shortgrass Prairie." The whimsical illustrations accompanying this lively story are unusual in that they are set on wooden veneers.

Ketteman, Helen. (1995). *Luck With Potatoes*. Illustrated by Brian Floca. New York: Orchard Books. Set in a Tennessee mountain, *Luck With Potatoes* features Clemmon Hardigree whose streak of bad luck changes into a streak of wondrous good luck when he plants potatoes in Cow Hollow. His fortune, however, is not won lightly, but the story of its acquisition will surely make the reader smile. Of particular fascination are the mountain cows Clemmon milks. "They have holes in their ears and their back legs are longer than their front ones." Walking uphill is no problem but walking downhill is a bit problematic. The solution to the difficulty is unique. Floca's watercolors capture the adventurous spirit of the story.

McKissack, Patricia, C. (1992). *A Million Fish . . . More or Less*. Illustrated by Dena Schutzer. New York: Alfred A. Knopf. "Hugh Thomas had just tossed his line into the water when Pap-Daddy and Elder Abbajon came rowing out of the gauzy river fog. They were swapping bayou tales, just like they had for years." Their stories match the tallest of the tall . . . in '03 the pair found a 500 pound turkey, a lamp that had been burning for 350 years, and the biggest, meanest cottonmouth ever seen! When challenged by Hugh, the pair admit that their facts were "more or less" correct. What is a certainty, they told the boy, is the strange things that happen on the Bayou Clapateaux. And indeed they do!

Sanfield, Steve. (1996). *The Great Turtle Drive*. Illustrated by Dirk Zimmer. New York: Alfred A. Knopf. This windie opens with a question from a former cowboy, "Want to hear a true story about how I made and lost a million dollars before I was old enough to vote?" As a young man and a true son of the Old West he tasted turtle soup. When he discovered how much it cost, the cowboy began to dream big financial dreams. So he undertook a turtle drive— a huge turtle drive of 20,000 turtles from Texas to Kansas City. What follows is a hilarious account of the drive and how his dreams of great wealth were dashed on the long, weary way.

Stanley, Diane. (1996). *Saving Sweetness*. Illustrated by G. Brian Karas. New York: G. P. Putnum's Sons. Sweetness is the littlest girl orphan in mean old Mrs. Sump's care. "Mrs. Sump doesn't much like seein' the orphans restin' or havin' any fun, so she puts 'em out to scrubbin' the floor with toothbrushes." "Enough," thought Sweetness and she hit the road! In a fake display of hysteria, Mrs. Sump sends the Sheriff out to look for the child. Three times the little girl has to rescue the hapless Sheriff from himself out in the desert, the last from the dreaded Coyote Pete. Still the lawman continues in his blissful self-delusion that he is saving Sweetness. Finally the little girl talks him into adopting her and the others at the orphanage! But there is more in store.

Yorinks, Arthur. (1994). *Whitefish Will Rides Again!* Illustrated by Mort Drucker. New York: HarperCollins Publishers. Another story based on the premise that life does not have to be ruled by a gun is Arthur Orinks, *Whitefish Will Rides Again!* "Who's Whitefish Will? Why, he's just about the best danged sheriff that ever lived. That's who." Whitefish Will, with the strength of 40 mules, is so good he rassled all the rustlers out of town and there was nothing left for him to do. In his forced retirement, Will took up ranching and the harmonica. Bart, mean Bart, meanwhile made his appearance in town, scaring folks into submission. Only Whitefish Will was deemed to be a match for the crook. When he whipped out his harmonica, he was indeed. Bart and his gang hightailed it out of town escaping the noise, never to be seen again!

Texts Cited

Dorson, R. M. (1971). *American Folklore*. Chicago: University of Chicago Press.

6

The Heavens

The heavens—the moon, the sun, and the stars—have always fascinated people. This is evident by the large numbers of folk tales available about these various bodies. Nor has the fascination waivered with the advance of scientific knowledge. There are some contemporary stories about the heavens that may well endure for as long as the tales that preceded them.

Earth and Sky

The sky must have appeared solid to the ancients. There are certainly many peoples, the Norse, the Greeks, and Native Americans among others who believed that the sky was the dwelling place of the gods.

According to many creation myths, earth and sky were joined at one time and had to be separated. This was frequently both a lengthy and painful process. The Maori of New Zealand have a story that in the beginning, Papatuanuku, the Earth Mother (Papa) who is also the first woman, lay beneath her husband, the sky or Ranginui (Rangi). Between them crept their many children longing for light. One of them, Tāne, god of the bush, eventually pried his parents apart by lying on his back and pushing the sky upward. Light came to the world. While they always knew this was to be their fate, the primal pair show continual grief at their separation. In the early morning Papa sends up mist to Rangi and he in turn sheds tears as rain. Even though Tāne was justified and his actions inevitable, he felt saddened by what he had done. As a way of comforting his father he decorated him with the sun, the moon, and the stars in the sky today known as the Milky Way.

In Egyptian mythology it is the Mother of all is who thought of as the sky. She had to be separated from her husband, also her brother, by their father, Shu and kept apart from him by the winds. Her story can be found in Mary Hoffman and Jane Ray's extensive text, *Sun, Moon and Stars*.

Gods of the Heavens

Ancient cultures had gods of the heavens. The Greeks (and Romans) would have told you that Artemis (or Diana) was goddess of the moon. Thoth, who was patron of science and literature, wisdom and invention was worshiped as a moon god by the Egyptians. In Sumeria, today known as Iraq, the "Queen of Heaven" was Inanna (ee-NAN-nah). Her dress was made of the stars, the rainbow became her necklace and the zodiac her waistband. On her head was a crown of the crescent moon. Besides being the ruler of the heavens, she was believed to control the clouds that gave water for the grain to grow; a singular power in a parched land. Inanna once visited her sister, Ereshkigal, goddess of the dead. In a decidedly dastardly act of malice Ereshkigal killed Inanna and hung her corpse on a stake. When this happened the moon disappeared from the night sky. After three days the water god sprinkled water on the corpse of the goddess resurrecting Inanna, whereupon she returned to the world and brought the moon back with her. This is the reason the moon waxes and wanes today.

Another interesting mythological belief relating to the heavens concerns the Norse Valkyries. These are warring maidens, virgins mounted upon horses wearing helmet and spear, who ride out to do the bidding of Odin, the All-father. The god desires to assemble as many heroes as possible to help him fight off the giants on the day of reckoning. He sends the young women out to choose who shall be slain in battle and subsequently take up residence in his great hall, Valhalla, until needed. When the Valkyries ride out, their armor sends a strange flickering light which flashes over northern skies. These lights are now called Aurora Borealis or Northern Lights.

The Moon

The moon with its ever changing shape and cold night light has inspired many superstitions, beliefs, and is the subject of interesting stories. Some of these stories are designed to explain the very existence of the moon, others account for the fact that it takes on different configurations each evening, and yet other tales are explorations of the idea of a dweller in that faraway region. Below are related just a few of these many beliefs and stories. A related text suitable for young readers is noted where available.

The Moon's Existence

San Bushman in South Africa. One fascinating story that both accounts for the moon's existence and for the fact that it has a different character over time comes from the San who were Bushmen and some of the earliest inhabitants of South Africa. A character dominant in their folklore and much revered is Mantis, a superhero and a kind of trickster. It was Mantis, say the bushmen, who threw an old shoe into the sky and it became the moon. As it rises each day it is colored red from the dust of the Southern African veldt. It is also cold like old leather. Bushman believed that the sun is jealous of the moon when it is full as it challenges the sun's brightness. With its sharp rays the sun mercilessly slices off bits from the moon until there is just a little left. Then the old moon cries, "Oh! Oh! Leave a little backbone for the children!" Remorseful the sun goes away and soon the moon starts growing back to its normal size so the process can start all over again.

Netsilik People. The Netsilik people who live along the coast above the Arctic Circle in one of the most remote and rugged parts of the world also have a story about how both Sun and Moon came to be. A brother and a sister decided that as penance for wicked behavior they would change into something else and settled upon heavenly bodies. The brother chased the sister around the snow hut where they lived until they rose into the sky. At that point the girl extinguished the torch her brother was carrying because he had been so reluctant to accept punishment. With her still lighted torch she became the Sun and warmed the world; the brother is cold because his flame no longer burns.

Greenland. A similar story to that told by the Netsilik people is told by the peoples of Greenland. In this iteration the sun and moon are mortals, brother, *Anninga,* and sister, *Malina*. When Malina was teased by her sibling beyond endurance, she placed her hands in some soot generated by a lamp and rubbed them on her brother's face. She then ran from her tormentor and became the sun; Anninga at her heels became the moon. The dark spots observable on the moon's face are the soot spots placed there in play that day by the children. Anninga circles the sun constantly in hopes of catching it but becomes fatigued in the last quarter. He then leaves his house to hunt for seals and is absent for a few days. He can eat well on the spoils of his chase upon his return and fattens up to become a full moon.

Moon Dwellers

Who or what lives in the moon? Beliefs about who does live in the orb tend to be culturally ascribed. The inhabitants most frequently described across different ethnic groups are a man, a woman, a hare, a rabbit, or a toad.

The Man (or is it the Woman?) in the Moon. Generally in the west the moon dweller is considered to be a man and according to one tradition this man is the Biblical Cain. He lives with a dog and a thornbush; the latter with its spikes and briars is emblematic of Cain's fall from grace. Alternatively the French would have told you in times past that it was another figure from the Bible, Judas Iscariot, who is the man in the moon transported to that cold and lonely place because of his treason.

Alternative explanations have the man being a Sabbath breaker who was picking up faggots on a Sunday. He met a handsome church goer on his way out of the woods who asked the woodcutter, "Do you not know that this is Sunday where all must rest from their labors?" Whereupon the woodcutter laughed and said, "Sunday on earth or Monday in heaven, it is all the same to me." The church observer then proclaimed that since the woodcutter did not value his day on earth he could stay in a moon-day in perpetuity. Now the man stands as a warning to all Sabbath breakers. A German variation of this story has the violator stealing cabbages on Christmas Eve. Now he has to hold his load for ever except for the anniversary of his theft, Christmas Eve, when he also turns around once.

Other European versions vary with respect to the nature of the lunar resident. A Polish view of the moon dweller is that he is a magician, a nobleman from Cracow, who resides above the earth, unable to return because of a pact he made with the devil. Krystyna Turska's *The Magician of Cracow* is a telling of this story that is well established in Polish folklore and believed to be based on the life of a real nobleman.

The Man in the Moon is not exclusively western however. He has an Asian counterpart who is generally a mean character in blind pursuit of riches. This is his undoing. Steve Sanfield has retold an Asian version of this individual in his engaging picture book, *Just Rewards.* In this tale two farmer neighbors could not be more different. One is gentle and kind, the other mean of spirit. When the gentle man finds an injured bird, he nurses it back to health despite the jeers of his fellow farmer. When the bird is cured he presents the farmer with a seed which when nurtured a season produces the most wondrous water melons. When opened they are found to contain spectacular pearls, diamonds, gold, and riches. The poor farmer had his just rewards. The mean farmer attempts a similar feat, but he had to resort to shooting a bird first so he could cure it. During the healing process he kept reminding the tiny creature he was expecting a just reward for his trouble. The seed provided when the bird left grew into a huge vine that stretched all the way to the moon. Once the mean man had climbed it to its full extent the vine withered, leaving the tyrant scowling and adrift. He is there still if you look!

The Chinese support a more positive and whimsical view of the lunar resident. He is known as *Yue-lao* and is reported to hold power over human marriages. Yue-lao is reputed to join together men and women by an invisible silken cord which never breaks while life exists. Tao Liu Sanders relates a story about the invincibility of this cord, actually a red invisible thread in this instance, in her informative and dramatic text, *Dragons Gods and Spirits from Chinese Mythology*. In the story called *The God of Marriage*, a mortal by the name of Wei tried to circumvent the destiny in store for him to no avail. Yue-lao has a counterpart in Chinese folklore, a fairy woman called *Chang-o* or "Goddess of the Palace of the Moon." She is known to sit on a gold throne attended by angels and a host of fairies each wearing light.

Less kind than Chang-o are the two pretty sisters of Chinese folk tale who lived in the moon embroidering exquisite designs on silk. They tired of the adoring and fascinated looks of the people on earth who watched them work, and so they asked their brother who lived in the sun to trade places. When he pointed out, quite reasonably, that they would be even more visible because the sun is out in the day time the girls had a ready answer. They would use their embroidery needles to prick the eyes of anyone who has the temerity to gaze upon them. And they do to this day!

The Maori of New Zealand, Hawaiians, and Native Americans also subscribe to the idea of the person in the moon being a woman. The folk lore belief of the latter people is that the woman is old and not a little bad tempered. She was out collecting water one night when the moon disappeared behind a cloud. She cursed it and was banished to live in its cold shores as a punishment.

The Hawaiian version of how the lunar occupant came to be a woman is also a sobering expose of the struggle women had to gain equal status with men. The central character is Hina, a beautiful goddess, who as a young woman lived in a cave under Rainbow Falls. She could make the best tapa cloth in all Hawaii. But the villagers selfishly imposed upon her to make their cloth. To compound her difficulties, Hina's husband railed against her when she failed to be a good wife. Hina, weary of this life and wanting to be able to enjoy the natural world she loved, sought out a place where she could be at peace. It took three journeys, the final one to the moon. Here she can make tapa cloth at her leisure and enjoy the world about her. The clouds that can be seen in the sky from time to time are really Hina putting out her cloth to dry! Jama Kim Rattigan has lovingly retold this tale in picture book format.

Ed Young has captured a Native American myth about the female inhabitant of the moon in a text he has called *Moon Mother*. The first mother, a spirit woman, lives in the moon after giving birth to a little girl. As a gift to men and animals, she was transformed into the heavenly feature. This story is also an explanation of why new born babies cry when they are born; they are protesting the premature separation of the first mother and child.

Another Native American tale available for children is about a woman being the occupant of the moon by James Riordan is called *The Woman in the Moon*. This slightly melancholy tale is of a beautiful Indian princess by name of Lone Bird who refuses all offers of marriage. As she ages and sees her parents getting ready to join the spirit world Lone Bird becomes sad. She fears being alone. One night when the princess sees the bright moon above she cries out to it that it is beautiful. If she could love the moon she would not be lonely. The Good Spirit took pity and conveyed Lone Bird to the moon. There she remains to this day lighting the time when people tell their stories around campfires.

The Hare (Rabbit) in the Moon. In the east the inhabitant of the moon is often believed to be a hare or a toad, and the story of how the animal ended up there is frequently touching. Both are often perceived to be pounding rice in a mortar.

During the days when he was a wandering hermit on earth, Buddha found himself lost in a forest. He was guided out of the woods by a kindly hare who would take no payment for his trouble save fine conversation. When they reached the edge of the forest, Sasa, the hare, commented that the man must be hungry, for pickings in that part of the world were slim. "Indeed, I am famished," replied Buddha. At this comment the hare offered himself as a meal and quickly built a fire for that purpose. Buddha could not contemplate such a thought and grabbed the animal by the ears and flung him into the sky and onto the moon. "In the future, let the world look up at night and see my friend, Sasa-in-the-Moon, and remember how noble a creature he was." Such is the legend from Ceylon that can be found in Geraldine McCaughrean's collection, *The Golden Hoard*.

Other tales about Hare are not quite so charming. The Hottentots of South Africa have a fable in which Hare is sent to earth by Moon to tell mankind that as she, Moon, dies and is restored so men and women shall likewise die and be restored. Hare either mistook the message or maliciously told the people that they would die as does the moon but unlike the moon would not rise again. When Hare told Moon what he had done, the lunar body became enraged and took up a hatchet to split her messenger in half. The weapon missed its mark but did cut open the animal's upper lip giving rise to the term "hare-lip." Hare retaliated by scratching Moon and leaving dark marks on her face. They are visible from time to time.

Hare can also be cunning as well as malicious. A tale demonstrating his wit comes from the first story of the third book of the *Panchatantras*, an ancient collection of Indian tales. In this tale the land is suffering a drought and a herd of elephants had traveled far looking for water. They came upon a placid lake, known as Moon Lake because of the way the orb was reflected in the water, and trampled all over the banks in their haste to get a drink. In their careless manner they squashed many warrens, killing and maiming the hapless inhabitants. The hares held a meeting to discuss their plight. One wise member suggested he had a plan to get rid of the beasts. He presented himself to the elephant king as the hare that lived in the moon. He was sent to tell his excellency to tell "the elephants that they must not come back to the lake or else the beams from the moon would be withdrawn. Everyone would be burnt in the constant sunshine." Feeling an apology was due, the king of the elephants went to the lake and dropped his trunk into the water. This disturbed the reflection of the moon in the lake which the chief elephant took as an indication of anger. He offered his profuse apologies and vowed never to return.

Sometimes it is a rabbit instead of a hare who is associated with the earth's moon. Many Native American peoples of North America such as the Cree of the northern plains and north woods of Saskatchewan and Manitoba know this creature as a trickster-hero and call him Great Rabbit. Douglas Wood has retold one of their many stories about Rabbit-in-the-Moon which explains, in addition, why Crane now has such long legs. Big, lumbering Crane is the only bird in the world who is willing to take a determined Rabbit to see the moon. This entails a long flight with the determined hero hanging on to Crane's legs for an extended period and stretching them in the process. From Rabbit's perspective the journey was worth it and more. When he arrived he "filled up his eyes with the beauty of the earth, and tried hard to keep his ears from trembling."

Tony Johnston also relates how Rabbit took up residence so far above the earth in a story she titles *The Tale of Rabbit and Coyote*. Rabbit is not driven in this tale by fine motives though! Once, one full-moon night, Coyote was tricked by Rabbit. Angry Coyote gave a spirited chase but was again (and again and again) fooled by wily Rabbit who eventually took refuge up a ladder and in the moon. So, "that is why, to this very day, Coyote sits gazing at the moon. And now and then he howls at it. For he is still *very* furious with Rabbit." Bold, vibrant colors are used in the folk art illustrations of this tale of wit, deception, and humor.

The Toad in the Moon. A cautionary myth out of China explains that it is a toad that looks out on the earth when the moon is full. The story about how this came to be is relayed in Song Nan Zhang's *Five Heavenly Emperors*. Yi, who was the guardian of the god Dijun, incurred his master's disfavor and was banished from the sky. While he was happy living on earth with his wife, Chang-Er, he did not like the idea that as a mortal he would die. So he requested assistance from the goddess of magic medicines, the Queen of the West. She provided Yi with an elixir that would bring him to heaven. Chang-Er, however, consumed the drink and it was she who floated upwards toward the Moon Palace. At her entry she was turned into a toad and can be seen there still.

Other Moon Dwellers. Peruvians may tell you it is not a man, nor a woman, a hare, or a toad who lives in the moon, but a fox. Fox went into the heavens with his friend, Mole, who found the climb so far into space beyond him and fell back to earth. Ashamed at his failure, Mole still lives under the ground where no-one can see him. Lois Ehlert has presented this tale in a simple, vivid picture book format called *Moon Rope* with her trademark bold colors and distinctive, clean, dramatic shapes

Moon Miscellany

According to one story the people of Papua, New Guinea, do not believe that anyone lives in the moon but they have an explanation for the smudges all over it. Once there was only one woman in a village who had the power to make fire. Two boys curious about this power went to her hut while she was away to see if they could discover her secret. While poking about one of the children lifted a lid to a pot and unwillingly released the moon. It floated upwards and away into the sky. The boy attempted to catch it, but like a wet ball it was too slippery; and all that he could do was to leave his dirty hand prints all over it.

Besides entertainment, the moon was used for practical purposes. Its changing configuration was employed as a form of measurement by ancient peoples. One version of how this came to be is described by Jeanette Winter in the picture book, *The Girl and the Moon Man*. In this particular iteration a girl lives alone with her father and tends his reindeer. Because she is lonely during the winter nights the girl plays a flute. So enchanted by the sound is the moon that he comes down and tries to take her back with him to the sky. The girl thwarts his efforts through the help of a magic old stag and her own winsome mischief. When the weary moon could see he was going to be beaten, he had to promise many things to obtain his release—guiding people over the night plains, measuring the year, and lighting up the night sky.

The moon was a significant entity in the folk lore of the Native American. Each full moon of a lunar month was given a name to describe the essence of the period. Perhaps the most well known is a typical term for September which is often referred to as a Harvest Moon.

Jamake Highwater has explored the Native American belief that the moon is the guardian of man in his sophisticated text, *Moonsong Lullaby*. The dust jacket explains, "the Moon is thought to soothe the sleep of the Sun as she makes her path across the night sky." As the Moon sings to the people of the campfire many things happen—the men and women give thanks for the bounty of the earth, the animals sleep, the moonlight shepherds the mushrooms growing in the cool damp, and grandmothers talk of the old days. "Their stories speak to us across the years of things we must know." Startling photographs accompany this lullaby, a tribute to the traditions and family life of the Native American.

The moon was typically viewed as a friendly force in the lives of people, perhaps because of its role in helping people measure time as noted above and because it provides a soft light in the dark night sky. Amanda Walsh has captured these feelings in her retelling of an English folk tale she has named *The Buried Moon*. In this haunting version Walsh manages to evoke the atmosphere of a fireside telling. The story begins with the "Hidden Folk, Bogles, Dead Things and Night Demons" who fear light and terrorize night travelers venturing too close to the marshlands. The Moon attempts to save hapless visitors to the bog, but is herself entrapped by it's ugly inhabitants. When she fails to appear as expected at New Moon, the Wise Old Woman directs the villagers to her stony resting place where they can rescue the trapped orb.

While the moon is willing to come to earth, she is also willing to take things from earth. In the ancient Egyptian *Book of Respirations*, the goddess Isis is described as fervently wishing that the soul of her brother, Osiris, will rise to heaven in the disk of the moon. The moon is regarded as a suitable medium since it does not absorb souls as the earth absorbs bodies. In South America the Saliva Indians have pointed out the moon as a paradise since there exists no mosquitoes on that orb. Another enchanting tale of unknown origin is that everything that is misused on earth such as time, wealth, vows, and intentions unfulfilled are saved and treasured on the moon. The poet, Alexander Pope, was to write that the moon was home to all lost things such as the brains of heroes!

One of the more puzzling phenomena to the ancients was the lunar eclipse. Such events were typically regarded with fear because it was frequently thought to be the beginning of the destruction of the world. Some cultures assumed that there was an evil or angry being eating the moon—in India it was a serpent, in China a dragon, and Native Americans stated it to be dogs tearing at her flesh thereby accounting for the characteristic red color. The ancient Scandinavian *Eddas*, a collection of poetry, records a monster eating the moon by name of Managermer who stains the air with blood as he rips at the lunar body. A typical response to the eclipse was the making of a lot of noise by gongs and bells to scare away the oppressor. As such activities were successful, continuation of them was reinforced!

An interesting footnote with respect to lunar eclipses comes to us from history. During his last expedition to America, Christopher Columbus was captured by natives who refused to replenish his expedition. The crusty sailor, aware that an eclipse was at hand, threatened to deprive the people of light if they did not supply him with provisions. At first the people were indifferent to the demand; but when the moon disappeared as Columbus said it would, they brought the needed supplies along with profuse apologies. The date was March 1, 1504.

Miscellaneous Picture Books and Illustrated Texts: Moon

Bess, Clayton. (1983). *The Truth About the Moon*. Illustrated by Rosekrans Hoffman. Boston: Houghton Mifflin. When a curious little boy, Sumu, tried to catch the moon and put it in a bottle, he failed. In desperation he asked his sister to tell him the truth about the moon, wondering about its many faces. "You silly-silly! There is only one moon . . . . our pa told me so." But Pa's story had holes; he could not explain where the moon went in the daytime. When Sumu went to Ma, her story about the moon was also enchanting but her explanation was likewise wanting. Finally, the anxious little boy went to see the wise old man of the village. He admonished Sumu not to seek all the answers as that would take the magic out of life. But he was not the wise old man for nothing. He recognized it was time for curious, clever Sumu to go to school. When Sumu arrived he found to his great pleasure the moon was there to greet him! This text is an enchanting mix of folk tales bound together by a little boy's quest for understanding.

Milord, Susan. (1996). *Tales of the Shimmering Sky*. Illustrated by JoAnne Kitchel. Charlotte, VT: Williamson Publishing. Milord's text is bigger in scope than just moon stories as she takes a broad look at all natural phenomenon of the heavens. She has devoted considerable space to the moon, however, including tales about it from diverse cultures. There is a version of the Indian Buddhist, Hare in the Moon, for example, and another on how the foolish people of Chelm tried to capture its light. In addition, Milord has provided the young reader with interesting miscellany (why the moon is called blue and tips on how to remember if the moon is waxing or waning!) In addition, she provides descriptions of some experiments the budding scientist can undertake. Milord's text is a curious and successful mixture of scientific and folk tale.

Contemporary Moon Tales

As noted above, the heavens have not ceased to fascinate the contemporary mind nor has our scientific understanding of them dimmed our fanciful notions. A number of modern authors have developed stories in the tradition of folk tales about the creation of the moon and the special role it has in the lives of people.

Berger, Barbara. (1984). *Grandfather Twilight*. Illustrated by the author. New York: Philomel Books. *Grandfather Twilight* who "lives among the trees" has a responsible job. "When the day is done he closes his book, combs his beard, and puts on his jacket." He takes one glowing pearl from the endless string he has in his wooden chest and walks with it in his hand. The pearl grows larger and larger and larger until he reaches the sea. He gives it to the silence above the water and there it glows, luminous in the dark, as the moon. *Grandfather Twilight* can go home to bed. Berger has extended her spare text with tender and marvelous illustrations.

Davol, Marguerite W. (1997). *Batwings and the Curtain of Night*. Illustrated by Mary GrandPré. New York: Orchard Books. This contemporary folk tale features a rather whimsical woman who goes by the name of "The Mother of All Things." She creates the earth and all that is upon it with a swing of her skirts or a shake of her hand. Her satisfaction with the light world and the creatures upon it is dimmed when she realizes that her creation needs darkness from time to time. This the "Mother of All Things" achieves by weaving ferns and branches into a curtain to create night. All is well. All is well until the living creatures find the darkness too compelling and begin to complain. But the "Mother or All Things" is finished with her work and she leaves it to the creatures themselves to figure out how to make the curtain less oppressive each evening. It is the lowly bat and the owl who do so by unwittingly creating a moon and stars. This well-told tale is rather lengthy and would appeal to older children.

Field, Susan. (1993). *The Sun, the Moon and the Silver Baboon*. Illustrated by the author. New York: HarperCollins Publishers. Field's book with rhythmical, repetitive language tells of the evening a star came loose from the heavens, tumbled to earth, and became tangled in the branches of a tree. An anxious moon called for help, "I cannot leave the sky without all my stars." No animal or bird could shift it. "The owls couldn't pull quite hard enough, the insects could not eat enough, and the foxes couldn't think of anything to do!" The hyenas only laughed when the star called to them. Disturbed by the fuss, the brown baboon padded down to see what was going on. "Like a shadow he climbed the tree and loosened the tangled tail" and freed that star. A grateful moon gave him a coat as silver as moonlight, and he now shines as bright as any star!

Ryder, Joanne. (1991). *The Bear in the Moon*. Illustrated by Carol Lacey. New York: Morrow Junior Books. Joanne Ryder's story is an explanation as to why the moon has phases. It features a curious bear who lived long, long ago when the earth was new and all that was at the top of it was sea. She goes to the moon, discovers it is made of ice that she can run, rest, and hide upon, pleasures hitherto unknown. She then sends the ice down to earth for the other bears to enjoy but diminishes the moon in the process. Sadness is replaced by pleasure when it is discovered the moon will replenish both itself and the earth.

Reeves, James. (1971). *How the Moon Began*. Illustrated by Edward Ardizzone. London: Abelard-Schuman. This Grimms' tale about how the moon began has been retold by James Reeve. "Once upon a time there was no moon. The nights were as black as black." When four brothers from the land of Exe went to the land of Wye, they discovered there the night was not black but only half dark. They discovered the illumination to be the moon which the mayor had bought for two pounds ten and hung on an oak tree. They carried it home and all was well. But one by one the men died and insisted they take a share of the moon to their grave with them. It went with them to the underworld where the light began to cause trouble. Saint Peter had to intervene. He took the moon away and tossed it into the heavens where it is there to this day.

The Sun

Most cultures revered the sun as a giver of both light and heat. This heavenly body was also regarded as something of a mystery since it disappeared at night and reappeared in the morning seemingly reborn. For this reason the fabulous phoenix, a bird of Egypt with red and gold plumage that reputedly builds its own funeral pyre and throws itself into the flames, only to be born again from its own ashes, serves as a symbol for the sun. Like the mythical bird, the sun seems to die in its own fires at night and then rise again the next morning.

Most cultures had sun gods to worship. The ancient Greeks paid homage to Helios who rode a chariot pulled by four horses from east to west. He would sink into the sea each night and then float in a gold cup down the River Ocean to take up his journey once more at his starting place. Helios would be accompanied in his nightly sojourn by the all the stars except those two constellations known across the heavens. Ra, supposed ancestor of all the Pharaohs, and the Egyptian solar god was likewise revered. He was conceived as being born as a child each day and dying each day as an old man. He then entered the underworld and deprived the world of light until reborn in the morning.

A similar story is told as part of Russian mythology. Three women goddesses known as the Zorya—Dawn, Twilight, and Midnight—attend the sun-god who rides through the sky each day on his horse bringing light and warmth to the earth. The Zorya rule a magical island to which the sun-god returns every evening. At day break when the sun-god is ready to leave, Dawn opens the gates of heaven to let him leave; Twilight lets him in again on his return. Over the course of the day the god of light and sun becomes an old man but is reborn in the night as a new baby. Further information on the Russian Zorya can be found in Kris Waldherr's stunning text, *The Book of Goddesses*.

Sometimes the sun moved too quickly and according to ancient story had to be reminded that it need not go so fast. In Margaret Mayo's collection called *When the World Was Young* the sun is depicted as an adversary in a Polynesian tale. It skipped across the sky making the days short. No one had sufficient time to work and the children never had enough time to play. Maui, the demi-god, trickster figure, is credited with slowing down this process and thereby allowing enough time for both play and rest. But the children, needless to say, were not satisfied as there never seemed to be enough time to finish one last game.

One of the phenomenon of the heavens that would have been difficult for pre-scientific peoples to explain would have been the solar eclipse. Seminole Indians of the American southeast believed that the toad-frog had come along and was biting the sun and would continue to do so until it disappeared. For this reason, toad-frogs were scared away with loud noises.

Finally, there are flowers known for their adoration of the sun. One such plant is the sunflower and it is the subject of a rather poignant story from Greek folklore. Clytie was an ocean nymph who loved the god Apollo to distraction. She would sit outdoors all day pining and facing the sun as he journeyed across the sky. For his part Apollo felt no attraction to the hapless nymph. Eventually Clytie was changed into a heliotrope or sunflower, the flower that is forever turned toward and chasing the sun.

Africa. Tololwa Mollel's *A Promise to the Sun* is more a tale about the be-havior of bats than it is about the sun, but it is entertaining. The drought that seized the earth when it was new meant the land shriveled up. When the birds and visiting cousin Bat drew lots to see who would journey in search of rain, it was the visitor who won the thankless task. Bat had to search the heavens and plead with the moon, stars, clouds, wind, and sun for the needed moisture. Sun extracted a promise for her participation . . . . that a cool nest be built in the greenest patch in the forest for her so she could rest at night. Bat willingly agreed as did the parched birds on his breaking of the news. But they broke their word when the time came. Ashamed, Bat crept into a cave and refused to come out in the daytime when the sun could see him. And there he stays to this day!

Australia. An ancient Australian story, set in Dreamtime before there were people on earth, claims that the sun was born when Emu and Eagle had a quarrel in the dark. In frustration Eagle flung Emu's egg into the sky; it broke and the yoke caught fire. Biame, the Great Spirit, was amazed at how beauti-ful the earth looked in the light and he urged the spirit helpers to collect more wood for the fire. And so it has been to this day. When the flames blaze their hottest it is midday and when the fire glows to embers it is evening. Aware that many animals slept through the daylight hours, Biame asked the kook-aburra to laugh its loud laugh soon after the morning star is hung in the sky to awaken sleepy heads. A version of this tale is to be found in Margaret Mayo's collection of creation and pourquoi tales called *When the World Was Young*.

China. The Chinese used to say that there were once ten suns who spent their days in a mulberry tree. They took turns lighting the earth but one day decided to climb the heavens altogether. The immense heat they generated began to ravage the world, so the gods called for the divine archer, Yi. He shot them all out of the sky; all but one—the one that can be seen today. A variant of this tale is available in picture book format called *Er-Lang and the Suns* by Tony Guo and Euphine Cheung.

Eskimo. A particularly enchanting Eskimo tale is related by Bernard Em-ery and titled *How Snowshoe Hare Rescued the Sun*. In this well known story "in a time long past," the demons who lived below the earth decide to steal Sun to keep themselves warm in the upcoming winter. The next day when the animals of the tundra are suffering in the total darkness they begin to plan, somewhat acrimoniously, to restore Sun to the sky. Strong Bear and Fast Wolf both fail in this mission and it is up to unassuming Snowshoe Hare to try. A dramatic chase with the demons about to tear him from limb to limb ends when Hare kicks and fragments the Sun into the sky. One piece becomes the moon, others zoomed up to become all the Stars in the Milky Way! Spring comes to the tundra and the demons, banished to the cave by the light, are not seen again.

Another delightful story about how the sun is retrieved from a thief and is once again restored to the animal people is retold from the Haida oral tradition by Jamie Oliviero entitled *The Day the Sun Was Stolen*. When the world was new Raven molded all animals from clay giving Fish shiny scales, Beaver a flat tail, and Bear a very thick coat. Bear found the furry covering a burden since he was always hot. He resolved to steal the sun to cool down the world. This act had far reaching consequences for all other creatures now enduring endless gray and cold. They are saved by a brave child who ingeniously tricks Bear into releasing the sun.

Native American. The sun did not always have equal access to the animal people or animal people to it. Long, long ago when the earth was new it was the animals who decided when it was day and when it was night. The Creek Indians tell us that the daytime animals used their magic to keep the sun in the sky for days on end. But every so often the night time animals would triumph and keep the sky dark for as long as possible. This state of affairs was obviously unsatisfactory, if not untenable. The animals met. Using Racoon's tail as a model, Chipmunk suggested a compromise. Noting that Racoon's tail was divided into equal sections of dark and light, he wondered if the days and nights could not be likewise. And so it was. And so it is to this day. A retelling of this tale can be found in Susan Milord's text, *Tales of the Shimmering Sky*.

Sometimes, so the stories claim, it was necessary to go and steal a piece of fire from the sun to bring both heat and light to the world. Susan Roth has retold a Cherokee myth she has called *The Story of Light* that features the humble spider as the creature who does just that. The animal people have grown tired of banging into one another in the dark and hold council to see who should go and get some sun. Both Possum and Buzzard try and each fail, so tiny little Spider sets off with a clay pot she had fashioned. Slowly she brought back the sun to the animal people, following her thread back to the west and lighting her way with the sun pot. Tucked inside the creation myth are a couple of pourquoi stories. "Even today Possum shuns the sun; he still has a tail with no fur; and Buzzard has a head with no feathers; and Spider's webs still look like sun's rays; and pots are still dried slowly in the shadows before they are baked in a hot oven."

The Stars

Stars were important in people's lives. They served as a supposed guiding force and as a means of navigation.

Luck or good fortune was frequently assumed as a given for an individual when he or she was born under a star in the ascendant or moving to its highest place in the heavens where it is most easily observed. Sighting a star that appears to shoot across the sky is also generally regarded as an omen of good luck. This is particularly so if the person who sights the star makes a wish before it fades from sight.

This belief is akin to another; that since stars contain the soul of man, shooting stars are on their way to animate new children being born on earth. Another similar and comforting belief is that each time a person dies a new star is born in the heavens. The bereaved has only to look up into the night sky to see an apparently new and twinkling body to know that the loved one is safe and sending a message home to that effect.

According to Homer, "the stars were sent by Zeus as portents for mariners." Certainly many peoples have used the stars to guide their way. The early Phoenicians as they ploughed their sea trading routes around the Mediterranean and the Maoris on their southern migration in 840 A.D. to New Zealand, serve as two examples.

There are many stories in folklore about how an individual star or a group of stars known as a constellation came to be. Frequently, they are believed to have been placed by a god. At other times they were considered the handiwork of tricksters who created the world. Yet another explanation is that stars are people for whom the life on earth was too difficult and they took up another form.

Constellations

Constellations are groups of stars that often have an identifiable shape. Many of these constellations were named by ancient peoples according to these configurations, and there is astonishing similarity in the perception of individual cultures of these star groupings. For instance, the six or seven stars frequently referred to as the Pleiades represent six or seven young girls in a number of cultures from Australia to Japan to Greece. Because of the movement of the stars over the centuries, the original configuration that inspired the name may not be quite so apparent to the current observer.

Sometimes it is the trickster who created the earth who saw to it that the constellations were placed in the heavens. Harriet Peck Taylor relates a Wasco Indian tale based on this premise. "Many moons and many moons ago," Coyote lived in a canyon by a swift-running river. Fascinated by the stars, the animal person skillfully builds and climbs a ladder to the heavens to discover their secrets. From his vantage point on the moon Coyote uses his bow and arrow to rearrange the stars into the shapes of himself and his friends—Bear, Owl, Mountain Lion, etc. Upon his return to earth, Coyote rejoices in his handiwork and announces it to all through a howl, "*Oweowowooooah*," that calls through canyons and mesas. Then the animals crawl, slither, splash, and soar in response to the call and celebrate the event with a lavish feast and celebration.

The names used below to identify constellations or stars are those used by the ancient Greeks whose culture is the foundation of Western cultural thought and expression.

The Pleiades. The Pleiades are a closely spaced group of seven stars, six of which are so bright as to be visible without a telescope. At one time the Pleiades was only one star, and a boastful one at that according to an ancient Polynesian tale. He was brighter than all the stars around him, and they tired of his chatter of being the most dazzling and the most beloved of them all. Finally Tane-mahuta, the god who reigned over celestial lights decided to call him to account by banishing the brash star from the sky. Garnering up support from nearby stars Aldebaran and Taurus, the threesome chased Pleiades across the heavens. Guessing their intent, the young star welled up to such a point that he burst and became instead the six (or seven) of today. A retelling of this story is to be found in Susan Milord's *Tales of the Shimmering Sky*.

The Pleiades were named by the Greeks for the seven daughters of Atlas. According to an ancient legend they were all vigorously but unsuccessfully pursued by a mighty hunter, Orion, who was a young man of immense stature and beauty. Distressed by the chase, the girls called to Zeus who changed them into pigeons and then into a constellation. Only six of the sisters are visible, as Electra chose not to look down on the earth since she could see that Troy, the city founded by her son, Dardanus, was in ruins.

For his part, Orion's life was one of unrequited love. He was unsuccessful with women and goddesses both. Artemis, the goddess of the hunt had him killed to her sorrow. He was changed eventually into a constellation where he has a girdle, sword, club, and lion's skin. The daughter's of Atlas continue to torment him today as they fly before him in the heavens.

Another Greek legend has it that the seven daughters of Atlas were humiliated by their father's task of bearing the world on his shoulders, punishment for taking part in a revolt against the gods of Olympus. Maia, the goddess of spring, and her sisters mourned their father's fate so much that the gods turned them into doves. The birds flew to the highest heaven and then became the seven stars now known as the Pleiades.

Other cultures see the constellation in a different fashion. The Dutch claim they are a baker and his six daughters; whereas the Roumanians refer to this cluster as a hen and a brood of chickens. Yet another story about the seven stars is told by the Vietnamese; they are thought of as weavers and shine brightly as the all powerful Jade Emperor's daughters. The least bright star visits the earth as a young girl, falls in love with a poor mortal, releases him from the clutches of a wealthy miser with the help of her sisters, but ultimately is forced by her father to return to heaven. She has been able to live on earth only because fairy time and mortal time differs; a moment in the sky is months on land. This poignant story is told by Lynette Dyer Vuong in her collection of *Sky Legends of Vietnam*.

Some Native Americans call the Pleiades the Bunched Stars or the Lost Children. Paul Goble has relayed a rather poignant Blackfoot myth he calls *The Lost Children* that explains how this came to be. The tale is about the fate of six orphaned brothers who are neglected and scorned by the members of the tribe. Their only true companions are the camp dogs. Unable to tolerate their lives any longer the children choose to become stars in "The Above World." They can be seen there today, bunched together as they were in life. This is a cautionary tale about the need to treasure children as gifts from God.

The Hyades. The Hyades, six in number, were also considered to be the daughters of Atlas and half sisters of the Pleiades. Zeus left the tender Dionysus, the god of wine, in their care when he was a baby and their reward for their careful attention to the deity was to be set among the stars. They were subsequently known as the rainy stars since they set in early May and November in the morning and evening when it is frequently raining.

Ursa Major. Ursa Major or "The Great Bear" is rich in folklore. One Greek tradition has it that the bear is Callisto ("most fair"), the daughter of a king. Which king is disputed, either King Lycaon or King Nycteus. Callisto was not only fair but chaste and determined to remain a virgin. Zeus, chief among the gods of the Greek pantheon saw the lovely Callisto out hunting one day and he fell in love. A son, Arcas, was born of their forced union. Hera, Zeus' wife, angry and jealous turned the maiden into a bear and tried in time when Arcas was grown to have the innocent lad shoot his mother when hunting. Zeus snatched his former lover away, placing her among the stars where she earned her name "The Great Bear." Callisto was in time joined by her son who became known as "The Lesser Bear." Thwarted Hera, appalled at the honor to her rival, appealed to Poseidon to forbid the Bears to descend into the ocean as other stars do. They are the only constellations not to set below the horizon or to bathe in the ocean's waters.

Stefan Czernecki and Timothy Rhodes relate another folk tale, this time of Russian origin about Ursa Major which they call *Bear in the Sky*. Once upon a time a big brown bear who loved to dance is wounded. The gypsy couple who nurse him back to health determine the bear will make them wealthy. Indeed, it comes to pass. A princess, who will smile only when she can dance in the arms of a bear, bestows much gold and silver upon Zanko and Zora when they present her with the dancing animal. The couple's delight turns to horror when they find the Princess intends to keep the bear. When he refuses to dance further, the frustrated girl tears off his sparkling vest and flings it into the dark sky, leaving behind a stairway of stars. The bear climbs the stars and can be seen to this day dancing upon them in the star constellation of Ursa Major or "The Great Bear."

Perseus. Perseus and his exploits are now immortalized in a constellation of the same name and have been given voice in a text by Warwick Hutton.

The hero was born of a union between the god Zeus and Danae. Once Danae's father, Acrisius, learned that he would be killed by the child his daughter was carrying, he dispatched mother and son in a chest to sea, expecting the waves to do their worst. But the chest washed up on the island of Seriphos and was pulled ashore by a fisherman called Dictys who protected the pair. Dictys' brother was the ruler, and a cruel one at that, of the island. In time he tricks Perseus into seeking the head of the dreadful gorgon, Medusa.

Medusa had once been a great beauty and she had boasted about her physical charms, stupidly comparing herself with the goddess Athena. Medusa was particularly proud of her hair which the offended goddess changed into a head of hissing snakes. From then on anyone who looked upon this terrible creature was turned into stone.

Perseus avoided being petrified with the assistance of Athena's shield, a shiny piece of armory that reflected images as would a mirror. He killed Medusa as he looked in the reflection using a special sword provided by Hermes. A pair of winged sandals, an invisible helmet, and a *kibisis* or bag to carry the head, gifts from the Stygian nymphs, were also put to good use.

On his way home Perseus rescued an unfortunate maiden, Andromeda, who was about to be sacrificed, and made her his wife. As the pair flew over the Libyan desert some drops from the severed head Perseus was carrying fell to the ground and turned into snakes. Today the abundance of snakes in Libya is traced to this event!

The prophecy that Perseus would be the cause of his grandfather's death was fulfilled once the gorgon had been delivered to Athena and the invaluable gifts had been restored to their owners. On his way back to Argos, Perseus stopped to participate in some funeral games. He accidentally killed Acrisius when he threw a discus that veered around and struck his father. Oracles were devastatingly accurate.

The North Star and the Big Dipper. The North Star together with the group of stars nearby forms a configuration known as the Big Dipper.

The North Star has been used for many thousands of years as a navigation guide, since unlike most stars it appears always to be in the same place. It is also very bright and easy to identify. The Norse know this star as the "World Nail" because of its role in keeping the heavens fixed.

The Big Dipper is known as the drinking gourd in African American history and folklore, and this constellation has a very special place in their culture. The star cluster was a guide for those desperate slaves seeking freedom as they traveled at night and slept in the day heading toward Canada. Jeanette Winter has captured this dramatic experience in a picture book entitled *Follow the Drinking Gourd*.

Paul Goble has retold a lovely and ancient Cheyenne explanation he calls *Her Seven Brothers* of how the big dipper came to light up the sky and to circle the stationary North Star. The story has a feel of enchantment since the young Indian heroine can talk to the animals. An accomplished seamstress, she makes fine clothes for the seven brothers she has never seen. The Indian maiden does subsequently take up residence with her siblings and is happy until the chief of the Buffalo nation demands her hand. Seeking to protect her from the herd, the brothers take the young woman up a tree and they all mount the heavens from its tip. From thence they become stars that can be seen to this day. Terri Cohlene has retold a version of the tale she has named *Quillworker*.

In some cultures the big dipper is seen as a cart or a chariot moving around the polestar. In Germany the "Heavenly Cart" carries a man by name of Hans Dumkin who offered hospitality to Christ despite his own impoverished state. Since he had had no chance to act upon a desire to travel, Christ gave him his own cart and Hans became the star Alcor. Now the man (star) can travel throughout eternity and beyond!

The Milky Way. The Milky Way is a glowing band of stars within the billions of stars that comprise our galaxy or star system, and its name comes from its milky-looking strip appearance at night. Perhaps because it is such a dramatic looking system in the sky, the Milky Way is the most commonly referred to group of stars in the galaxy in folk tales. The Norse refer to it as "Freyja's (FRAY-ah's) necklace" after an ancient goddess who presided over the living and the dead. She was never seen without a beautiful shining necklace given to her by the dwarves who mine precious metals and gems.

The Milky Way is described in many cultures as the stairway to heaven or to the spirit world. Seminole Indians of the Southeast, people who settled in what is now Florida, thought of it as the way to the City of the West. The term in their language for the band of starlight is *so-lo-pi-he-ni* which means "spirit way" or "the Milky Way for human souls." The people believed it shined brightest when one of their honorable tribal members dies, as the stars are lighting the path of the traveling Seminole. Sometimes the traveler may be able to use "the Big Dipper," which is situated along the Milky Way. It appeared to the people as a boat which could be used to convey the good souls to the City in the Sky from which they never return.

Similarly the Vietnamese believe that it is along the Milky Way that one must walk to meet the Vietnamese ruler of all gods and spirits, Ngoc Hoàng, the Jade Emperor. Ngoc Hoàng and the Milky Way feature in Sherry Garland's *Why Ducks Sleep on One Leg*.

Stories that involve the Milky Way usually refer either to its function or its creation. Some of the stories about the latter are part of wider creation tales; the stars were formed about the time the earth was made. Alternatively, others are the story of the creation of the constellation itself, an event that happened independently of the formation of the world.

Creation of Milky Way. A particularly lovely version of how the Milky Way was created comes from the San Bushmen in Southern Africa. These are people whose culture was at its height when the white people arrived on the African continent. They have a story about a lonely girl who was waiting for her lover among the hunters who were late coming home one dark evening. As she huddled over the fire longing for her companions to return she had an idea. Placing her hands into the ashes uncaring of the pain the act caused her, she lifted a handful into the air and threw it into the sky. The white wood ash became the Milky Way and provided light to guide the hunters home.

Joseph Bruchac and Gayle Ross have retold a Cherokee story about the formation of the constellation called *The Story of the Milky Way*. It is set, as are many folk tales, "long ago when the world was new and there were few stars in the sky." People depended on corn, stored in bins behind their homes, for their food. Thus, the old man and the old woman were dismayed when they found their supply down by handspan. "Surely no one in the village would steal from the elders!" It was their beloved grandson who discovered that a great spirit dog was creeping in the dark and leaving tracks and cornmeal scattered behind him when he ate his fill. On the advice of the Beloved Woman, the villagers frightened the strange creature away the next night and he ran across the sky. The white cornmeal spilling from his mouth remained behind as a band of light, each grain becoming a star that twinkles to this day. Virginia Stroud, the illustrator and a Cherokee-Creek by birth has preserved her traditions in her art work supporting this mysterious tale.

Function of the Milky Way. Outside of being a bridge for souls seeking the spirit land, the function of the Milky Way is not always a happy one. One of the most widely told legends in Asia involves this galaxy. Tom Birdseye has a version he calls *A Song of Stars*. It is the story of a weaver, Chauchau, Daughter of the Emperor of the Heavens, who lived in a small house perched on the edge of a star. She falls in love with Newland who tends oxen and sings soft songs only they can hear. The lovers abandon their work when they marry and "duty was replaced by soft kisses." Angered, the Emperor of the Heavens separates the two, decreeing they will be allowed to cross the river of stars or milky way and meet only once a year on the seventh night of the seventh month.

In a Native American version of the Cinderella story retold by Rafe Martin the Milky Way is invoked. Termed *The Rough-Face Girl* in this story because of the injuries sustained when pushed into the fire by her sisters, the youngest of three daughters is able to capture the great hunter known as the Invisible Being. It is *The Rough-Face Girl* alone of all the village maidens who can see him and beauty in the nature about her. It is the innate goodness of the scarred and lonely maiden that attracts the Invisible Being whose bow is the rainbow and the Milky Way his sled runners. When the pair are married, "they lived together in great gladness and were never parted."

Individual Stars

Planet Venus or Lileken, the Orphan Star "At dawn the planet Venus appears in the east as the morning star. At nightfall it is the evening star in the west." The African Masai call this star Kileken, the orphan boy. Not until it is too late does the old man connect the disappearance one night of a bright star from the night sky with the arrival of a little orphan boy who "traveled count-less miles in search of a home." Life becomes easy for the old man after the arrival of Kileken; all the chores are completed effortlessly by the boy and his cattle thrive in the flaming drought. But no questions must be asked. When the old man cannot contain his curiosity any longer he loses the son he never had.

Stars that Come to Earth. It is seldom that stars venture to leave the heav-ens once they are there, although there is the odd tale which suggests this does happen. Stars take up a new form on earth either because they are weary of a celestial life or they wish to help someone. *The Orphan Boy* by Tololwa Mollel and referred to above, is an African folk tale that describes such an event.

Barbara Juster Esbesen has also retold a tale about a star that was tired of hanging in the sky. *The Star Maiden* comes to a young warrior in a dream begging for a place on the lovely, peaceful earth. He promises her she can take any form and rest where she wishes. But nothing pleases her—not the rose in which she chooses to live on the prairie or the blue flowers near the buffalo herd. After *The Star Maiden* returns to the sky she discovers her reflec-tion in a pond and, enchanted, calls upon her sisters to join her in a resting place. Today, this maiden and her friends can be found as luminous water lilies whose petals shine in the sun.

Texts Cited

Berger, B. (1984). *Grandfather Twilight*. Illustrated by the author. New York: Philomel Books.

Birdseye, T. (1990). *A Song of Stars*. Illustrated by Ju-Hong Chen. New York: Holi-day House.

Bruchac, J. & Ross, G. (1995). *The Story of the Milky Way*. Illustrated by Virginia A. Stroud. New York: Dial Books for Young Readers.

Carlstrom, N. W. (1992). *Northern Lullaby*. Illustrated by Leo and Diane Dillon. New York: Philomel Books.

Cohlene, T. (1990). *Quillworker*. Illustrated by Charles Reasoner. Vero Beach, Florida: The Rourke Corporation, Inc.

Czernecki, S. & Rhodes, T. (1990). *Bear in the Sky*. Illustrated by Stefan Czernecki. New York: Sterling Publishing Co., Inc.

Davol, M. W. (1997). *Batwings and the Curtain of Night*. Illustrated by Mary GrandPré. New York: Orchard Books.

Ehlert, L. (1992). *Moon Rope*. Illustrated by the author. New York: Harcourt Brace Jovanovich.

Emery, B. (1993). *How Snowshoe Hare Rescued the Sun*. Illustrated by Durga Bernhard. New York: Holiday House.

Esbensen, B. J. (1988). *The Star Maiden*. Illustrated by Helen K. Davie. Boston: Little, Brown and Company.

Field, S. (1993). *The Sun, the Moon and the Silver Baboon*. Illustrated by the author. New York: HarperCollins Publishers.

Field, E. (1973). *Eskimo Songs and Stories*. Illustrated by Kiakshuk and Pudlo. New York: Dell Publishing Co., Inc.

Garland, S. (1993). *Why Ducks Sleep on One Leg*. Illustrated by Jean and Mou-Sien Tseng. New York: Scholastic, Inc.

Goble, P. (1993). *The Lost Children*. Illustrated by the author. New York: Bradbury Press.

Goble, P. (1988). *Her Seven Brothers*. Illustrated by the author. New York: Bradbury Press.

Guo, T. & E. Cheung. (1994). *Er-Lang and the Suns*. Illustrated by Karl Edwards. New York: Mondo Publishing.

Highwater, J. (1981). *Moonsong Lullaby*. Photographs by Marcia Keegan. New York: Lothrop & Lee Shepard Books.

Hoffman, M. (1998). *Sun, Moon and Stars*. Illustrated by Jane Ray. New York: Dutton Children's Books.

Hutton, W. (1993). *Perseus*. Illustrated by the author. New York: Margaret K. McElderry Books.

Johnston, T. (194). *The Tale of Rabbit and Coyote*. Illustrated by Tomie dePaola. New York: G.P. Putnam's Sons.

Martin, R. (1992). *The Rough Face Girl*. Illustrated by David Shannon. New York: G.P. Putnams' Sons.

Milord, S. (1996). *Tales of the Shimmering Sky*. Illustrated by JoAnne E. Kitchel. Charlotte, VT: Williamson Publishing.

McCaughrean, G. (19976) *The Golden Hoard*. New York: Simon & Schuster.

Mollel, T. M. (1992). *A Promise to the Sun*. Illustrated by Beatriz Vidal. Boston: Little, Brown & Company.

Mollel, T. M. (1990). *The Orphan Boy*. Illustrated by Paul Morin. New York: Clarion Books.

Oliviero, J. (1995). *The Day the Sun Was Stolen*. Illustrated by Sharon Hitchcock. New York: Hyperion Books for Children.

Oughton, J. (1992). *How the Stars Fell into the Sky*. Illustrated by Lisa Desimini. Boston: Houghton Mifflin Company.

Rattigan, J. K. (1996). *The Woman in the Moon*. Illustrated by Carla Golembe. New York: Little, Brown and Company.

Reeves, J. (1971). *How the Moon Began*. Illustrated by Edward Ardizzone. Great Britain: Abelard-Schuman.

Roth, S. L. (1990). *The Story of Light*. Illustrated by the author. New York: William Morrow and Company, Inc.

Ryder, J. (1991). *The Bear in the Moon*. Illustrated by Carol Lacey. New York: Morrow Junior Books.

Sanders, T. T. L. (1980). *Dragons Gods & Spirits from Chinese Mythology*. Illustrated by Johnny Pau. New York: Peter Bedrick Books.

Sanfield, S. (1996). *Just Rewards*. Illustrated by Emily Lisker. New York: Orchard Books.

Taylor, H. P. (1993). *Coyote Places the Stars*. Illustrated by the author. New York: Bradbury Press.

Turska, K. (1975). *The Magician of Cracow*. Illustrated by the author. New York: Greenwillow Books.

Vuong, L. D. (1993). *Sky Legends of Vietnam*. Illustrated by Vo-Dinh Mai. New York: HarperCollins Publishers.

Waldherr, K. (1995). *The Book of Goddesses*. Illustrated by the author. Hillsboro, Oregon: Beyond Words Publishing, Inc.

Walsh, A. (1991). *The Buried Moon*. Illustrated by the author. New York: Houghton Mifflin.

Winter, J. (1988). *Follow the Drinking Gourd*. Illustrated by the author. New York: Alfred A. Knopf.

Winter, J. (1984). *The Girl and the Moon Man*. Illustrated by the author. New York: Pantheon Books.

Wood, D. (1998). *Rabbit and the Moon*. Illustrated by Leslie Baker. New York: Simon & Schuster.

Young, E. (1993). *Moon Mother*. Illustrated by the author. Willa Perlman Books.

Zhang, S. N. (1994) *Five Heavenly Emperors*. Montreal: Tundra Books.

Children's Author Index

Index